CW01522425

# Do Not Forget!

A Collection of Old Celtic Sayings, Blessings, Curses and Proverbs of Irish and Scottish Origin for Today

JAMES F. HATCHER III

Copyright© 2015.  James F. Hatcher III

All rights reserved.

ISBN-13: 978-1507757086
ISBN-10: 1507757085

Available from Amazon.com, CreateSpace.com,
and other retail outlets

www.CreateSpace.com/5285680

Published by The Masonic Press.
Find more related titles on our website:

# masonicpress.com

Printed by CreateSpace, Charleston, SC
An Amazon.com Company

# Dedication

This book is dedicated to our daughter, Catherine Grace, for her undivided attention to and constant love of all things Celtic.

Especially the music.

"May those who love us, love us.
And those that don't love us,
May God turn their hearts.
And if He doesn't turn their hearts,
May he turn their ankles,
So we may know them by their limping."

*~The Author's Favorite Celtic Blessing*

"May the curse of Mary Malone
and her nine, blind, illegitimate children
chase you so far over the Hills of
Damnation that the Lord himself
can't find you with a telescope!"

*~The Author's Favorite Celtic Curse*

# Contents

# Foreword

Growing up in and being from that part of the United States called East Tennessee, you learn very quickly how your family heritage is very, very deep-rooted in Scots-Irish tradition. It is, or was recently (until the invasion of the "fernurs"), a part of growing up in this part of the world.

It bothers me that people I know, who are of Scots-Irish descent, have no general clue that they are. Friends have asked me, "What clan do I belong to or do I?" Many times, I say, "Your Last Name..."

There is a movement currently underway, whereby, people are seeking out their family heritage, and it appears that this is something that is becoming important again. Saints be praised! It is a sad thing when one does not know, or especially care, where they came from. As we progress down that road of modern technology, we slowly but surely are ridding ourselved of the knowledge and customs of our ancestors and their great deeds, trials and tribulations. It is said that History repeats itself, and we need not wait until it does to remember why it does.

This book is written for our daughter, Catherine Grace or"Catie" in hopes that she will learn and pass down that knowledge wisdom and advice herein contained to those who come after her. As a decendant of the Clan Campbell on three of four of her grandparents' sides (and 41 other Scottish Clans and of the Irish in many ancestral lines), she has shown promise in taking to the old ways. She is the only 9 year-old I know, who recognizes and can sing along with Ronnie Drew and the Dubliners...at least in this part of the world! She can sing The Mountain Dew and Finnegan's Wake (her favorites) and hold her own on both! She, like her brothers, also has a kilt (Ancient Campbell) and wears it at Highland Games. They all three have an interest in their heritage, and hopefully, they always will. I know not what the future brings, but I do know that it does, and will always, involve family. No matter if hard times come, and they will, or things are good, and they will be, the traditions of family and one's heritage will keep alive the memories of the past and hope for the future.

The following content is a compilation of sayings from both the Irish and the Scottish, which are often no longer heard in families, but should be. It applies to anyone, but that closeness bears down on those of Celtic descent when Gaelic is spoken, and rings echoes of our dearly departed parents and grandparents, who many of us long to hear argue, demand and insist that we do it the "correct way" in that Scots-Irish tone and fashion. Their voices are now silent, but their memories live on for their descendants to preserve through the traditions, recollections, and customs of both Tara and the Western Highlands.


Ne Obliviscaris,
The Author

# 1 Celtic Blessings and Sayings

A man's best friend is his mother until he meets his wife.

A Merry Christmas this December
To a lot of folks I don't remember.

Always remember to forget
The friends that proved untrue.
But never forget to remember
Those that have stuck by you.

Always remember to forget
The things that made you sad.
But never forget to remember
The things that made you glad.

Always remember to forget
The troubles that passed away
But never forget to remember
The blessings that come each day.

Leave the table hungry.
Leave the bed sleepy.
Leave the table thirsty.

And if you inherit a donkey,
May she be in foal.

Ar dheas Dé go raibh a anam.
*May his/her soul be on God's right hand.*

Arrah, may God give you sense.

Bless those minding cattle,
And those minding sheep,
And those fishing the sea
While the rest of us sleep.

Bless you and yours
As well as the cottage you live in.
May the roof overhead be well-thatched
And those inside be well matched.

Bottoms up or bottoms down,
Either way no one will frown.

Codladh sámh.
(Pronounced Cuh-lah sawve)
*Sleep well.*

Dear Lord,
Give me a few friends
who will love me for what I am,
and keep ever burning
before my vagrant steps
the kindly light of hope...
And though I come not within sight
of the castle of my dreams,
teach me to be thankful for life,
and for time's olden memories
that are good and sweet.
And may the evening's twilight
find me gentle still.
Dia leat!
(Pronounced Dee-ah lath!)
*Bless you!*
(when someone sneezes)

Faol saol agat, gob fliuch, agus bás in Éirinn.
*Long life to you, a wet mouth, and death in Ireland.*

For each petal on the shamrock
This brings a wish your way
Good health, good luck, and happiness
For today and every day.

For the test of the heart is trouble
And it always comes with years.
And the smile that is worth the praises of earth
Is the smile that shines through the tears.

From the County of Meath,
the health of the hag.
Not of her but her drink
is the reason we brag.

Go maire sibh bhur saol nua.
(Pronounced Guh mah-reh shiv voor say-ol nu-ah)
*May you enjoy your new life.*

Go mairir is go gcathair.
(Pronounced Guh mah-rir is guh gaw-hir)
*May you live and may you wear it out.*

Go n-eírí an bóthar leat.
*May the road rise with you.*

Go n-eirí an t-ádh leat.
(Pronounced Guh nye-ree on taw laht.)
*Good luck to you.*

Go raibh míle maith agat!
(Pronounced Guh rev mee-lah maw og-ut)
*That you may have a thousand good things!*

God between us and all harm.

3

God bless all here.

God bless the corners of this house
And be the lintel blessed.
Bless the hearth, the table too
And bless each place of rest.
Bless each door that opens wide
To stranger, kith and kin;
Bless each shining window-pane
That lets the sunshine in.
Bless the roof-tree up above
Bless every solid wall.
The peace of Man,
The peace of love,
The peace of God on all.
God bless the corners of this house,
And be the lintel blest,
And bless the hearth and bless the board,
And bless each place of rest,
And bless each door that opens wide
To stranger as to kin,
And bless each crystal window pane
That lets the starlight in,
And bless the rooftree overhead
And every sturdy wall.
The peace of man,
The peace of God,
The peace of love on all.

Good health,
good life,
good beer!

Grant me a sense of humor, Lord,
The saving grace to see a joke,
To win some happiness from life,
And pass it on to other folk.

Health and a long life to you.

Land without rent to you.
A child every year to you.
And if you can't go to heaven,
May you at least die in Ireland.

Health and life to you;
The mate of your choice to you;
Land without rent to you,
And death in Eirinn.

Here's a toast to your enemies' enemies!

Here's health to your enemies' enemies!

Here's that we may always have
A clean shirt
A clean conscience
And a punt in our pocket.

Here's to a fellow who smiles
When life runs along like a song.
And here's to the lad who can smile
When everything goes dead wrong.

Here's to a long life and a merry one.
A quick death and an easy one.
A pretty girl and an honest one.
A cold beer-and another one!

Here's to Hell!
May the stay there be
as fun as the way there!

Here's to it and for it and do it again.
For those that get to it
And refuse to do it,
May never get to it
To do it again.

Here's to the grey goose
With the golden wing;
A free country
And a Fenian King.

Here's to you and here's to me.
May we never disagree.
But should we start to fight and 'cuss,
Here's to me.

Here's to you and your friends and family.

Here's to you and yours
And to mine and ours.
And if mine and ours
Ever come across to you and yours,
I hope you and yours will do
As much for mine and ours
As mine and ours have done
For you and yours!

Here's to you both, a beautiful pair
On the birthday of your love affair
Here's to the husband and here's to the wife
May yourselves be lovers for the rest of your life.

Here's to you, as good as you are.
Here's to me as bad as I am.
As good as you are and as bad as I am,
I'm as good as you are, as bad as I am.

I complained that I had no shoes
Until I met a man who had no feet.
I drink to your health when I'm with you,
I drink to your health when I'm alone,
I drink to your health so often,
I'm starting to worry about my own.

If God sends you down a stony path,
may he give you strong shoes.

If you lie, may you lie only to keep a friend
If you cheat, may you cheat only death
If you steal, may you steal your lover's heart
If you drink, may you drink deeply
of the joy of your new life together.

Ireland, it's the one place on earth
That heaven has kissed
With melody, mirth,
And meadow and mist.

Ireland, sir, for good or evil,
No other place under Heaven.
And no man can touch its sod
Or breathe its air without becoming
Better or worse.

It's easy to be pleasant when life flows by like a song.
But the man worthwhile is the one who can smile
When everything goes dead wrong.

Like the goodness of the five loaves and two fishes,
Which God divided among the five thousand men,
May the blessing of the King who so divided
Be upon our share of this common meal.

Love is blind but marriage restores eyesight!

Maith thú
(Pronounced Maw hoo)
*Good on you.*

May a mouse never leave your meal bag with a tear in its eye!
May all your troubles be little ones
and all your little ones be trouble free.

7

May all your ups and downs be under the sheets.

May brooks and trees and singing hills
Join in the chorus, too.
And every gentle wind that blows
Send happiness to you.

May God bless the ground you walk upon.
May God grant you a generous share of eternity.

May God level the road for his soul.

May neighbours respect you,
Trouble neglect you,
The angels protect you,
And heaven accept you.

May peace and plenty be the first
To lift the latch on your door,
And happiness be guided to your home
By the candle of Christmas.

May the best day of your past be the worst day of your future.

May the blessing of the great rains be on you,
may they beat upon your spirit
and wash it fair and clean,
and leave there many a shining pool
where the blue of heaven shines,
and sometimes a star.

May the blessing of the rain be on you — the soft sweet rain.
May it fall upon your spirit so that all the little flowers may spring
up, and shed their sweetness on the air.
May the blessings of each day be the blessings you need most.

May the blessings of light be upon you,
Light without and light within.
And in all your comings and goings,

May you ever have a kindly greeting
From them you meet along the road.

May the blessings of Saint Patrick behold you.

May the crows never pick your haystack.
If you inherit a donkey, may she be in foal.

May the enemies of Ireland never meet a friend.

May the face of every good news
And the back of every bad news
Be toward us.

May the frost never afflict your spuds.
May the leaves of your cabbage always be free from worms.
May the good earth be soft under you
when you rest upon it,
and may it rest easy over you when,
at the last, you lay out under it,
And may it rest so lightly over you
that your soul may be out
from under it quickly,
and up, and off,
And be on its way to God.

May the grass grow long on the road to hell for want of use.

May the hinges of our friendship never grow rusty!

May the Irish hills caress you.
May her lakes and rivers bless you.
May the luck of the Irish enfold you.
May the blessings of Saint Patrick behold you.
May the joys of today
Be those of tomorrow.
The goblets of life
Hold no dregs of sorrow.

May the leprechauns be near you,
To spread luck along your way.
And may all the Irish angels,
Smile upon you St. Patrick's Day.

May the leprechauns dance over your bed and bring you sweet
dreams.

May the light of heaven shine on your grave.

May the Lord keep you in his hand but never close his fist tight on
you.

May the luck of the Irish
Lead to happiest heights
And the highway you travel
Be lined with green lights.

May the luck of the Irish possess you.
May the devil fly off with your worries.
May God bless you forever and ever.

May the most you wish for
Be the least you get.

May the rains sweep gentle across your fields,
May the sun warm the land,
May every good seed you have planted bear fruit,
And late summer find you standing in fields of plenty.

May the road rise to meet you.
May the wind be always at your back.
May the sun shine warm upon your face.
And rains fall soft upon your fields.
And until we meet again,
May God hold you in the hollow of His hand.

May the roof above you never fall in,
And those gathered beneath it never fall out.

May the saddest day of your future be no worse
Than the happiest day of your past.

May the smile of God light you to glory.

May the strength of three be in your journey.

May the wind always be at your back.

May the wind you break always blow down wind.

May there always be work for your hands to do,
May your purse always hold a coin or two,
May the sun always shine warm on your windowpane,
May a rainbow be certain to follow each rain,
May the hand of a friend always be near you,
And may God fill your heart with gladness to cheer you.

May there always be work for your hands to do.
May your purse always hold a coin or two.
May the sun always shine on your window pane.
May a rainbow be certain to follow each rain.
May the hand of a friend always be near you.
May God fill your heart with gladness to cheer you.

May there be a fox on your fishing hook
And a hare on your bait
And may you kill no fish
Until St. Brigid's Day.
May there be spring enough in your life to outlast the winters;
May there be guitars and drums enough to lift your spirits
whenever you need it;
May you be gentle enough to comfort those who are hurting,
But revolutionary enough to bring heaven to those who need it
now.

May there always be a leprechaun near you
to bring out laughter and
dance and the child in you.
And may God always have room enough
for you in the palm of his hand!

May there be rain at your funeral.

May those who love us love us.
And those that don't love us,
May God turn their hearts.
And if He doesn't turn their hearts,
May he turn their ankles,
So we'll know them by their limping.

May you always come more than you go.

May you always have
money in your pocket,
a woman to love,
and a smile on your face.

May you be at the gates of heaven an hour before the devil knows
your dead!

May you be poor in misfortune,
Rich in blessings,
Slow to make enemies,
And quick to make friends.
But rich or poor, quick or slow,
May you know nothing but happiness
From this day forward.
May you escape the gallows, avoid distress, and be as healthy as a
trout.

May you have food and raiment,
A soft pillow for your head,
May you be forty years in heaven
Before the devil knows you're dead.

May you have length with your days,
and strength with your step,
and may each season have a reason
to celebrate your faith in mankind!

May you have rye bread to do you good,
Wheaten bread to sweeten your blood,
Barley bread to do you no harm
And oatmeal bread to strengthen your arm.

May you have the health to wear it.

May you have the hindsight to know where you've been,
the foresight to know where you're going,
and the insight to know when you're going too far.

May you have warm words on a cold evening,
A full moon on a dark night,
And the road downhill all the way to your door.

May you have warm words on a cold evening,
A full moon on a dark night,
And the road downhill all the way to your door.

May you have:
No frost on your spuds,
No worms on your cabbage.

May your goat give plenty of milk.

May you live as long as you want, and never want as long as you
live.

May you live long,
Die happy,
And rate a mansion in heaven.

May you live to be a hundred years,
With one extra year to repent!

May you never bear the heavy load of an empty stomach.

May you receive mercy and grace,
death without sin
and may the righteous gone before you
receive their share of Eternal Glory.

May you see him/her in heaven.

May your day be touched
by a bit of Irish luck,
brightened by a song in your heart,
and warmed by the smiles of the people you love.

May your heart be warm and happy
With the lilt of Irish laughter
Every day in every way
And forever and ever after.

May your home always be too small to hold all your friends.

May your neighbors respect you,
Trouble neglect you,
The angels protect you,
And heaven accept you.

May your right hand always
Be stretched out in friendship
And never in want.
May your thoughts be as glad as the shamrocks.
May your heart be as light as a song.
May each day bring you bright happy hours,
That stay with you all year long.

May your troubles be as few and as far apart as my
Grandmother's teeth.

May your troubles be less
And your blessings be more.
And nothing but happiness
Come through your door.

Mo sheacht mbeannacht ort!
(Pronounced Muh hyawch(k)t mann-ach(k)t urt)
My seven blessings on you!

More power to your elbow.

Mothers hold their children's hands for just a little while...
And their hearts forever.

Murphy's Law:
Nothing is as easy as it looks.
Everything takes longer than you expect.
And if anything can go wrong,
It will at the worst possible moment.

Nár laga Dia thú
(Pronouncd Nawr lag-ah Dee-ah hoo)
May God never weaken you.

Now sweetly lies old Ireland
Emerald green beyond the foam,
Awakening sweet memories,
Calling the heart back home.

Peace on your hand and health to all who shake it.

Saol fada agus breac-shláinte chugat.
(Pronounced Say-ol faw-dah og-uss brack- hlawn-cheh ch(k)oo-at)
*Long-life and fair health to you.*

Sláinte chugat.
(Pronounced Slawn-cheh ch(k)oo-at)
*Good health to you.*

Sláinte go saol agat,
Bean ar do mhian agat
Talamh gan chíos agat
Leanbh gach bliain agat,
Is solas na bhflaitheas tar éis an tsaoil seo agat.
*Health during your life,*
*A wife of your choice to you,*
*Land without rent to you,*
*A child every year to you,*
*And the light of heaven after this world for you.*

Solas Mhic Dé ar a n-anam.
(Pronounced Suh-lass Vic Day err a nan-am.)
*The Light of the Son of God on her soul.*

St. Patrick was a gentleman
Who through strategy and stealth
Drove all the snakes from Ireland.
Here's toasting to his health.
But not too many toastings
Lest you lose yourself and then
Forget the good St. Patrick
And see all those snakes again.

Surely, a fine husband is he that flinches at the mere raisin' of his
wife's fair hand.

That you may never be left to die a sinner.

The blessing of God on you.

The Grace and Prosperity of God on you.

The health of all Ireland
and of County Mayo,
And when that much is dead,
may we still be on the go.

The Lord have mercy on his soul.

The words that I've said I meant when I spoke
and remember my words of wisdom
feck'em if you can't take a joke.

There are good ships
and there are wood ships,
the ships that sail the sea.
But the best ships are
friendships,
and may they always be.

There are only two kinds of people in the world,
The Irish and those who wish they were.

There comes a time when you must take the bull
By the tail and face the situation squarely.

Tis better to buy a small bouquet
And give to your friend this very day,
Than a bushel of roses white and red
To lay on his coffin after he's dead.

To live above with the Saints we love,
Ah, that is the purest glory.
To live below with the Saints we know,
Ah, that is another story.

To the doctor may you never hand any money,
And sweet be your hand in a pot full of honey.

We cannot share this sorrow
If we haven't grieved a while.
Nor can we feel another's joy
Until we've learned to smile.

What is Irish diplomacy?
It's the ability to tell a man to go to hell,
So that he will look forward to making the trip.

When we drink, we get drunk.
When we get drunk, we fall asleep.
When we fall asleep, we commit no sin.
When we commit no sin, we go to heaven.
So, let's all get drunk, and go to heaven!

When you reach the inn of death,
I hope it's closing time.

Wherever you go and whatever you do,
May the luck of the Irish be there with you.

Wishing you always...
Walls for the wind,
A roof for the rain
And tea beside the fire.
Laughter to cheer you,
Those you love near you,
And all that your heart may desire.

With the help of God, you'll pull through.

Your health one and all,
from one wall to the other,
And you outside there
speak up, brother!

You're not as young as you used to be.
But...You're not as old as you're going to be.
So watch it!

# 2 Celtic Marriage & Wedding Blessings

A child every year for you.
Health and life to you
The woman of your choice for you
A child every year for you
And may you die in Ireland.

Health to the men
and may the women
live forever.

Help and deliverance
and friendship of God
on you both.
God grant you a gradle of joy.
May your troubles be few
and your blessings plenty.

Love, life and happiness.
May your troubles be few
and your blessings plenty.

May you know nothing but happiness from this day forward.

May you marry an orphan.

May you never be sent to the gander paddock.

May you sleep in your man's dirty nightshirt and not rue it.

May your bodies please each other
like the stars do their Master.

May your neighbors respect you
May trouble neglect you
May the angels protect you
And may heaven accept you.

Sliocht sleachta ar shliocht bhur sleachta.
*May there be a generation of children on your children's children.*

Sweet be her hand on you as if it came from a pot of honey.

That you may never marry a whistling woman.
That your love knot be sealed with heaven's wax.

That your wife may knit for infants
and may her needles always click after dark.

You for me
and I for thee
and never another.
Your face turned to mine
and away from all others.

# 3 Celtic Curses

A child be within you forever unborn!

A death without a priest to him in a town without a clergyman!

A fox on you fishing hook!

A high windy gallows to him!

A mountain landslide down upon you!

A poisonous pain in you!

A red nail on the tongue that said it!

A red stone in your throat!

A stiff hanging hasty suitable rope round the thin throttle of this thieving villain, torturing and hanging and shaking and trembling on a rope!

After keening you infant!

And the day will come when he'll be cold and dumb and roast for eternity!

Bad cess (luck) to you!

Bad cess to him!

Bad luck on him!

Blast you to hell!

Briseadh agus brú ar do chnámha!
A breaking and crushing on your bones!

But may she still be alive till everyone is sick at the sight!

By my tongue may it get you!

Confusion on the money!

Curse of God on you!

Curse of the seven snotty orphans on you!

Damn your soul to everlasting hell!

Death and smothering on you!

Derangement and madness on his mind come soon!

Dysentery on you!

Evil,death short life to (name)!

Go hifreann leat!
*To hell with you!*

Go n-ithe an cat thú is go n-ithe an diabhal an cat!
*May the cat eat you, and may the devil eat the cat!*

Go n-ithe an tochas thú!
*May you be eaten by an awful itch!*

Go to the dickens!

Harm and death to you swarthy (name) in the middle of the field
may your horse kill you because of
what was small and worthless-a pair of guns though o'er a fence
thrown!

Hell roast him!

He's as greedy as a sow As the crows behind the plough- The
black man from the mountain, Shauneen Roo!

Horo, O minister who gave me two pence!

I bind you by grave injunctions of magic from the river, back to
the river!

I Call on you o stone to keep Breed below. She kept us short of
drink and on our house brought shame. And since, o Breed,
you're buried now Eternal thirst to you and drought!

I give you to the devil!

I loathe and detest the miserable bastards!

I pray for sorrow on the house!

I pray the powerful Creator that you may go as high as the shaft
of the missile and in the clouds of

heaven as any bird and may the death you gave my companion-
death at spear point-come also on you!

If your crop is tall, may your meitheal be small!

Imeacht gan teacht ort.
*May you leave without returning!*

In hell may you be because of your sins!

23

In the depths of the whirlpool with Oscar blowing and twenty-one demons each tearing you asunder!

Let it not be long till you die despite the son of god!

May (name) pay!

May (name) perish!

May a stich or convulsion strike you!

May Aeolus chase her into the harbors of Acheron down!

May all the goats in Gorey chase you staright to hell!

May all the Thieving fiends assail the thieving town of (name)!

May beef or lamb or veal be never seen in (name)!

May every day of it be wet for ye!

May Fire and brimstone never fail to fall in showers on (name)!

May god weaken you!

May he always be flying and straying naked through the world until death at spear-point takes him!

May he die roaring!

May he fester in his grave!

May he melt away like the froth of the river Fishes hate!

May he never have a day of luck!

May his death come on the rest of them down to the very last one!

May hound-wounding, heart-ache and vultures gouge her eyes!

May it do him no good only sorrow!

May old harry run away with him!

May savage dogs eat you one foot on a mountain!

May spears of battle destroy (name)!

May the cats eat the women!

May the curse of curses in sorrow prostrate you now!

May the curse of Mary Malone and her nine blind illegitimate children chase you so far over the Hills of Damnation that the Lord himself can't find you with a telescope!

May the devil cut the head off you and make a day's work of your neck!

May the devil damn you to the stone of dirges or to the well of ashes seven miles below hell and may the devil break your bones. And all my calamity and harm and misfortune for a year on you!

May the devil have your soul under guard there. For you treacherously swore that the head of the croppies was power whom you couldn't disparage!

May the devil make a fool of you!

May the devil roast the ___ off Him!

May the devil swallow him sideways!.

May the devil take him by the heels and shake him!

May the devil take your last shilling!

May the devil tear you!

May the entrails and mansion of pleasure out of this worm fall out!

May the gates of paradise never open to you!

May the lamb of God stir his hoof through the roof of heaven and kick you in the arse down to hell!

May the seven terriers of hell sit on the spool of your breast and bark in at your soul!

May the snails devour his corpse And the rains do harm worse May the devil sweep the hairy creature soon!

May there be guinea-fowl crying at your child's birth!

May there never be enough of your people to make a half-set!

May this insect get an illness that Hippocrates Cannot cure!

May you all go to hell and not have a drop of porter to quench your eternal thirst!

May you be afflicted with the itch and have no nails to scratch with!

May you be broken over the mason's cliff!

May you be mangled!

May you die without a priest in a town with no clergy!

May you fall in a nettle patch!
May you find the bees but miss the honey!

May you garner under Oscar's Flail!

May you have a little skillet, May you have little in it, May you have to break it, To find the little bit in it!

May you have no good luck and I recant the curse That you may die roarin' like Doran's ass!

May you have the runs on your wedding night!

May you marry a wench that blows wind like a stone from a sling!

May you marry in haste and repent at leisure!

May you melt off the earth like snow off the ditch!

May you never have a hearth to call your own!

May you not see the cuckoo nor the corncrake!

May your child not walk and your cow be flayed. And may the flame be bigger and wider which will go through your soul than the Connemara mountains if they were on fire!

May your choking come on you!

May your hens take the disorder, your cows the crippen and your calves the white scour!

May your spuds be like rosary-beads on the stalk!

May yourself go stone-blind so that you will not know your wife from a hay stack!

My curse attend (name). Her boats her borough and her fish. May every woe that mars man come dancing down upon her dish.

For all the thieves behind you from Slaneyu's banks to Shannon side are poor scholars, mind you, to the rogues you'd meet in (name)!

My curse ever upon Sweeney and my blessing on Eorainn!

My curse on you and Crossconnell and may it never be without a fool!

My curse on you and ruin to you, you lying thieving rascal!

Nine time sicker than the Ulstermen's illness let her be!

No butter be on your milk nor on your ducks a web!

O Jesus dear God and Father of the Lamb, who sees us in fetters and in bondage so hard, as you made us Christians between Friday and Monday, thus protect us and banish this scum from us!

Oh (name), may harm overtake you!

Or if be born may he not be like a Christian. A pigs snout on him and the mouth of a sheep. A beak of a duck that could dredge in the sludge. Lest he be a hangman that would hang the people!

Pissmircs and spiders be in your marriage bed!

Pursuing to them!

Rain and fire ill wind and snow and hard-frost follow her!

Scorn disgrace malediction by churches and bells!

She won't be here any other time I'll call!

Since you stole the sheep, you lying spoiler into hell I wish you to be tormented!

Six horse-loads of graveyard clay on top of you!

That you may be a load for four before the year is out!

That you may scratch a beggarman's back one day!

The anguished bankruptcy of the year to you!

The Boss of the ship underneath and the rest of the people being saved!

The crows' curse on you!

The curse of Cromwell on you!

The curse of his weapons upon him!

The curse of Jesus on you!

The curse of the crows on you!

The curse of the wretched and the strong on the one who gave Tattheration to him for a mule!

The curse of widows and orphans on you!

The death of the kittens to you!

The devil mend you!

The devil swallow him sideways!

The devil sweep him!

The fate of Ned's cock to you!

The Roasting of the salmon to the very end on you!

The sea cat and death-strangling to her!

The treatment of the boiled broken little fish to you!

The world will see that they won't have a day's luck and will disappear like the froth of the river!

To Halifax with him!

Trasna ort féin!
*Go across yourself!*
*(Go f@\*k yourself)*

Whoever put me into impotent grief And took my white tom-cat in secret from me. May the mice come in waves as his company and the rats from the kiln give him the pursuit!

Woe to you you dirty fellow You've filthied me!

You will be defeated in every engagement you take part in and in every assembly you attend you will be spat on and reviled!

You will go and live always in that place where the fishes and sprats live!

Your old frame dead and lifeless with never a stir. With none to wake your corpse your limbs without a shroud!

Your soul to the devil!

# 4 Celtic Toasts

A bird never flew on one wing.

A bird with one wing can't fly.

Always remember to forget
The troubles that passed away.
But never forget to remember
The blessings that come each day.

Athbhliain faoi mhaise duit!
(Pronounced Aw-vlee-an fee vosh-eh gwit)
*A prosperous New Year to you!*

Beannachtaí na Féile Pádraig oraibh!
(Pronounced Ban-awch(k)-tee nah Fay-leh Paw-rig ur-iv!)
*Blessing of St. Patrick's Day on you.*

Beimid ag ól!
(Pronounced Beh-mid egg ole)
*Let's be drinking!*

Céad Míle Fáilte! [IRISH GAELIC]
(Pronounced Kayd Mee-la Fall-cha)
*One hundred thousand welcomes!*

Ceud Míle Fáilte! [SCOTTISH GAELIC]
(Pronounced Kee-ud Mee-la Fall-cha)
*One hundred thousand welcomes!*

Croí folláin agus gob fliuch
(Pronounced Cree full-awn aw-gus gub fluch(k)
*May you have a healthy heart and a wet mouth!*

Don't put in the name of the person,
and the music is the same as in English.

Fad saol agat, gob fliuch, agus bás in Éirinn.
(Pronounced Fawd say-al aw-gut, gub fluch(k) aw-gus bawss in
Aye-rinn)
*May you have a long life, a wet mouth and may you be buried in Ireland.*

Go mbeirimíd beo ar an am seo arís.
(Pronounced Guh mer-i-meed byoh er an am shoh areesh)
*May we be alive at this same time again next year*

Health and long life to you,
land without rent to you,
a child every year to you,
and death in Old Ireland.

Here's to you and yours,
And to mine and ours,
And if mine and ours ever come
Across you and yours,
I hope you and yours will do
As much for mine and ours,
As mine and ours have done
For you and yours!

Here's to a long life and a merry one.
A quick death and an easy one.
A pretty girl and an honest one.
A cold pint, and another one!

Here's to a temperance supper,
With water in glasses tall,
And coffee and tea to end with
And me not there at all!

Here's to being single...
Drinking doubles...
And seeing triple!

Here's to health, peace and prosperity.
May the flower of love never be nipped
by the frost of disappointment,
nor shadow of grief fall
among your family and friends.

Here's to our wives and girlfriends…
May they never meet!

Here's to the land of the shamrock so green,
Here's to each lad and his darlin colleen,
Here's to the ones we love dearest and most.
May God bless old Ireland, that's this Irishman's toast!

Here's to women's kisses,
and to whiskey, amber clear;
Not as sweet as a woman's kiss,
but a darn sight more sincere!

I drink to your health when I'm with you,
I drink to your health when I'm alone,
I drink to your health so often,
I'm starting to worry about my own!

I have known many, and liked not a few,
but loved only one and this toast is to you.
If you're enough lucky to be Irish,
You're lucky enough!

It is better to spend money
like there's no tomorrow
than to spend tonight
like there's no money.

Lá Breithe Shona dhaoibh!
(Pronounced Law breh-heh hun-ah gweeve)
*Happy Birthday to you all!*

Lá Breithe Shona dhuit
Lá Breithe Shona dhuit
Lá Breithe, Lá Breithe
Lá Breithe Shona dhuit
*Happy Birthday to you,*
*Happy Birthday to you,*
*Happy Birthday, Happy Birthday,*
*Happy Birthday to you,*

Lá Breithe Shona dhuit!
(Pronounced Law breh-heh hun-ah gwit)
*Happy Birthday to you!*

Love is blind but marriage restore eyesight!

May a mouse never leave your meal bag with a tear in its eye!

May all your ups and downs be under the sheets.

May big headaches and little fevers be always far from you.

May God grant you many years to live,
for sure he must be knowing,
the earth has angels all too few
and heaven is overflowing.

May I see you grey and combing your grandchildren's hair.
May misfortune follow you the rest of your life, and never catch
up!

May neighbours respect you,
Trouble neglect you,
The angels protect you,
And heaven accept you.

May the doctor never earn a pound out of you.

May the face of every good news and the back of every bad news
be towards us.

May the good Lord take a liking to you...
But not too soon!

May the hinges of our friendship never grow rusty.

May the lilt of Irish laughter lighten every load.
May the mist of Irish magic shorten every road
 And may all your friends remember
all the favours you are owed!

May the Lord keep you in His hand
And never close His fist too tight

May the luck of the Irish
Lead to happiest heights
And the highway you travel
Be lined with green lights.

May the most you wish for is the least you get!

May the road rise to meet you.
May the wind be always at your back.
May the sun shine warm upon your face.
And rains fall soft upon your fields.
And until we meet again,
May God hold you in the hollow of His hand.

May the roof above you never fall in,
And those gathered beneath it never fall out.

May the roof over your heads be as well thatched
As those inside are well matched.

May the saddest day of your future
be no worse than
the happiest day of your past.

May those that love us, love us.
And those that don't love us,
May God turn their hearts.
And if he doesn't turn their hearts,
May he turn their ankles,
So we'll know them by their limping.

May you always have a clean shirt,
a clear conscience,
and enough coins in your pocket
to buy a pint!

May you be in heaven a full half hour before the devil knows your
dead.

May you be poor in misfortune,
rich in blessings,
slow to make enemies
and quick to make friends.
And may you know nothing
but happiness from this day forward.

May you die in bed at 95,
shot by a jealous spouse.

May you get all your wishes but one,
so that you will always have something to strive for!

May you grow old in the face
Be treasured and cared for with grace.

May you have all the happiness
and luck that life can hold
And at the end of all your rainbows
may you find a pot of gold.

May you have food and raiment,
a soft pillow for your head.
May you be forty years in heaven
before the devil knows you're dead.

May you have nicer legs than yours under the table before the
new spuds are up.

May you have rye bread to do you good,
Wheaten bread to sweeten your blood,
Barley bread to do you no harm
And oatmeal bread to strengthen your arm.

May you have the hindsight to know where you've been,
The foresight to know where you are going,
And the insight to know when you have gone too far.

May you have warm words on a cold evening,
a full moon on a dark night,
and a smooth road all the way to your door.

May you live all the days of your life.

May you live as long as you want
and never want as long as you live!

May you live to be 100 years, with one extra year to repent.

May you live to be a hundred years,
With one extra year to repent!
May your glass be ever full.
May the roof over your head be always strong.
And may you be in heaven half an hour
before the devil knows you're dead.

May your heart be light and happy,
May your smile be big and wide,
And may your pockets always have
a coin or two inside!

May your home always be too small to hold all your friends.

May your mornings bring joy and your evenings bring peace,
May your troubles grow less as your blessings increase!

May your pockets be heavy
Your heart be light,
And may good luck pursue you
Each morning and night.

May your right hand always
Be stretched out in friendship
And never in want.

My friends are the best friends
Loyal, willing and able.
Now let's get to drinking!
All glasses off the table!

Níl aon leigheas ar an ngrá ach pósadh.
(Pronounced Neel ane lie-ass er on nraw awch(k) poe-sah)
There's no cure for love except to marry.

Nollaig shona dhuit!
(Pronounced Null-ig hun-ah gwit)
Happy Christmas to you!

Sláinte
(Pronounced Slawn-che)
*Health! (Cheers)*

Sláinte an bhradáin agat.
(Pronounced Slawn-cheh on vraw-dawn ogg-ut)
*May you have the health of the salmon.*

Sláinte chuig na fir, agus go mairfidh na mná go deo.
(Pronounced Slaw-in-cheh chwig nah fir, og-uss guh mir-hig nah mnawh guh jo)
*Health to the men and may the women live forever*

Sláinte chuig na fir, agus go mairfidh na mná go deo.
*Health to the men, and may the women live forever!*

Sláinte go saol agat,
Bean ar do mhian agat.
Leanbh gach blian agat,
Is solas na bhflaitheas tareis antsail seo agat.
*Health for life to you,*
*A wife of your choice to you,*
*Land without rent to you,*
*A child every year to you,*
*And the light of heaven after this world for you.*

Sláinte!
(Pronounced slawn-cha)
*Cheers!*

Sliocht sleachta ar shliocht bhur sleachta.
*May there be a generation of children on the children of your children.*

That the tap may be open when it rusts!

The light of the Christmas star to you
The warmth of home and hearth to you
The cheer and good will of friends to you
The hope of a childlike heart to you
The joy of a thousand angels to you
The love of the Son and God's peace to you.

There are good ships,
and there are wood ships,
The ships that sail the sea.
But the best ships,

are friendships,
And may they always be.

To live above with the Saints we love,
Ah, that is the purest glory.
To live below with the Saints we know,
Ah, that is another story!

We drink to your coffin.
May it be built from the wood
of a hundred year old oak tree
that I shall plant tomorrow.

When money's tight and hard to get,
and your horse is also ran,
When all you have is a heap of debt,
a pint of plain is your only man.

Wherever you go and whatever you do,
May the luck of the Irish be there with you.

# 5 Celtic Proverbs in Gaelic

Ag duine féin is fearr a fhios cá luíonn an bhróg air.
*The wearer best knows where the shoe pinches.*

Aithníonn ciaróg ciaróg eile.
(Pronounced Ah-hneen kee-rogue kee-rogue el-eh)
*It takes one to know one.*

An áit a bhuil do chroí is ann a thabharfas do chosa thú.
*Your feet will bring you to where your heart is.*

An áit a mbíonn mná bíonn caint agus an áit a mbíonn géanna
bíonn callán.
*Where there are women there is talk, and where there are geese there is
cackling.*

An beagán, go minic, a fhágas rioc sa sparán.
*A little, often, leaves wrinkles in the purse.*

An bhean atá dóighiúil is furasta a cóiriú.
*A handsome woman is easily dressed.*

An lao ite i mbolg na mbó aige.
*He has eaten the calf in the stomach's cow. He has gone into debt on the assumption that future profits will clear the debt.*

An luífeása le mo mhuintirse?
*Would you like to be buried with my people?*

An rud a líonas an tsúil líonann sé an croí.
*What fills the eye fills the heart.*

An rud is annamh is iontach.
(Pronounced On rud iss an-niv is ee-on-tach(k))
*The thing that's seldom is wonderful .*

An rud ná cloiseann an chluas ní chuireann sé buairt ar an gcroí.
*What the ear does not hear will not worry the heart.*

An rud nach fiú é a lorg, ní fiú í a fháil.
*What is not worth seeking, is not worth finding.*

An rud nach leigheasann im ná uisce beatha níl aon leigheas air.
*What butter or whiskey does not cure cannot be cured.*

An tae nach bhfuil láidir, ní foláir dó bheith te.
*The tea which is not strong, has to be hot.*

An té a bhíonn siúlach, bíonn scéalach.
(Pronounced On tay a vee-on shoo-loch(k), bee-on skay-loch(k))
*He who travels has stories to tell.*

An té a bhíonn siúlach, bíonn sé scéalach agus an té a bhíonn scéalach bíonn sé bréagach.
*He who travels is talkative (full of stories), and he who is talkative has a*

*tendency to lie.*

An té a bhíonn thuas óltar deoch air, an té a bhíonn thíos buailtear cos air.
*He who is successful is celebrated with drink, he who is down is kicked.*

An té a dtéann cáil na mochéirí amach dó ní miste dó codladh go méanlae.
*He who gets a name for early rising can stay in bed until midday.*

An té a dtéann teist na mochóirí amach air ní cás dó codladh go headra.
*The person who gains the reputation of getting up early can sleep late.*

An té a luíonn le madaí, eiroidh sé le dearnaid.
(Pronounced On tay a lee-on le maw-dee aye-rogue shay le dar-nid.)
*He who lies down with dogs, gets up with fleas. If you mix with the wrong company, you'll pay for it.*

An té a thabharfas scéal chugat tabharfaidh sé dhá scéal uait.
(Pronounced On tay a hoo-rass skay-al ch(k)oo-at too-rig shay gaw skay-al oo-at)
*The person who comes with a story to you will bring two away from you.*

An té is ciúine is é is buaine.
*He who is silent is the stronger.*

An té is mó a osclaíonn a bhéal is é is lú a osclaíonn a sparán.
*The one who opens his mouth the most, it is he who opens his purse the least.*

An té is mó airgid is é is mó dúil ann.
*He who has the most money has the most regard, at least while he has it.*

An té ná faigheann an fheoil is mór an seó leis an t-anraith.
*He who does not get meat will get great satisfaction from the soup. The person that does not get the great prize, may be happy just to get something.*

An té nach bhfuil láidir, ní foláir dó bheith glic.
(Pronounced On tay noch(k) will law-dir, nee foh-lawr doh veh glick)
*He who is not strong must be clever.*

An té nach bhfuil láidir, ní foláir dó bheith in ann rith go tapa.
*He who's not strong, has to be able to run well.*

An té nach bpósann níl ach uaigneas dilte dósan.
*He who does not marry will be lonely.*

An té nach trua leis do chás, ná déan do ghearán leis.
*Don't go to him with your problem who has no sympathy for your case.*

An t-uan ag múineadh méilí dá mháthair.
*The lamb teaching its mother how to bleat.*

Ar mhaithe leis féin a níos an cat crónán.
*The cat purrs to please itself.*

Ar scáth a chéile a mhaireann na daoine.
(Pronounced Err scawh a ch(k)ale-ah a wir-enn na dee-neh)
*Under the shelter of each other, people survive.*

Ar scáth a chéile a mhaireas na daoine.
*People live in one another's shelter.*

Baineann an druncaeir an díon dá thigh féin agus cuireann ar thigh an tábhairne é.
*The drunkard takes the roof from his own house and puts it on the publican's house.*

Beagán a rá agus é a rá go maith.
*Say little but say it well.*

Bí go maith leis an ngarlach agus tiocfaidh sé amárach.
*Be good to the child and he will come to you tomorrow.*

Bíonn adharca fada ar na ba thar lear.
(Pronounced Bee-on ire-cah faw-dah ar na bah hawr lahr.)
*Far away cows have long horns. Far away hills are greener.*

Bíonn blas ar an mbeagán.
(Pronounced Bee-on bloss err on myah-gon)
*Though a small amount, it's tasty.*

Bionn ceann caol ar an óige.
*You cannot put an old head on the young.*

Bíonn chuile dhuine lách go dtéann bó ina gharraí.
*Everyone is sociable until a cow invades his garden.*

Bíonn fáilte agus fiche roimh chuireadh gan iarraidh.
*There is great welcome in an unsolicited invitation.*

Bíonn gach duine go lách go dtéann bó ina gharraí.
*Everybody is good natured until a cow goes into his garden.*

Bíonn gach tosach lag.
*Every beginning is weak.*

Bíonn grásta Dé idir an diallait agus an talamh.
*The grace of God is found between the saddle and the ground.*

Bíonn súil le muir ach ní bhíonn súil le tír.
*There's hope from the ocean but none from the grave.*

Capall an tsaoil an grá.
*Love makes the world go around.*

Capall na hoibre an bia.
*Food is the horse of work. Food is what keeps you going.*

Cé gur beag díol dreoilín caithfidh sé a sholáthar.
*Little as a wren needs, it must gather it.*

Ceannigh droch rud is bí gan aon rud.
*Buy a bad thing and be left with nothing.*

Céard a dhéanfadh mac an chait ach luch a mharú?
*What would the cat's son do but kill a mouse?*

Coimhéad fearg fhear na foighde.
*Beware of the anger of a patient man.*

Cuir síoda ar ghabhar ach is gabhar i gcónaí é.
(Pronounced Kwir shee-id-ah ar gow-er awch(k) is gow-er i go-nee aye)
*Dress a goat in silk and he still remains a goat; You can't make a silk purse out of a sow's ear.*

Cuir síoda ar ghabhar agus is gabhar i gcónaí é.
*Put silk on a goat and it is still a goat.*

Dá fhada an lá tagann an tráthnóna.
(Pronounced Daw aw-dah on law tog-ann an traw-no-nah.)
*No matter how long the day, the evening comes. No matter how bad
things are, they will end.*

Dá fheabhas é an t-ól is é an tart a dheireadh.
*Good as drink is, it ends in thirst.*

Dá ghile an t-éadach, is fusa é a shalachadh.
*The whiter the cloth the easier soiled.*

De réir a chéile a thógtar na caisleáin.
*It takes time to build castles.*

Déan an fál nó íocfaidh tú foghail.
*Make the fence or you will pay for the plunder.*

Dearmad bhean an tí ag an gcat.
*The cat benefits from the housewife's negligence.*

Dhá thrian den obair í an chosúlacht.
*Two thirds of the work is the semblance.*

Dia idir sinn agus an t-olc.
(Pronounced Dee-ah id-ir shin og-uss on tulk)
*God between us and all harm. When you hear bad news.*

Drochubh, drochéan.
(Pronounced Druch(k)-uv, druch(K)-ay-an)
*A bad egg, a bad bird.*

Faigh do bhean i gcóngar, ach i bhfad uait díol do bhó.
*Get your wife locally, but you sell your cow far away.*

Faigheann an tseanbhróg an tseanstoca.
*The old shoe gets the old stocking.*

Féasta anocht agus gorta amárach.
*A feast tonight and a famine tomorrow.*

Feileann spallaí do bhallaí chomh maith le clocha móra.
*Pebbles suit walls as well as big rocks.*

Filleann an feall ar an bhfeallaire.
(Pronounced Fill-an on fyal err on vyal-er-eh.)
*The bad deed returns on the bad-deed doer.*

Folíonn grá gráin.
*Love veils ugliness.*

Galar gan náire an tart.
*Thirst is a shameless disease.*

Giorraíonn beirt bóthar.
*Two people shorten the road; having a travelling companion makes the trip more enjoyable.*

Glacann drochbhean comhairle gach fir ach a fhear féin.
*A bad wife takes the advice of every man except her husband.*

Glaonn gach coileach go dána ar a atrainn fhéin.
*Every cock crows boldly in his own farmyard.*

Go gcoinní Dia i mbois a láimhe thú, agus nár dhúna sé a dhorn go teann choíche.
*May the Lord keep you in his hand and never close his fist too tight.*

Go n-ithe an cat thú is go n-ithe an diabhal an cat.
*May the cat eat you and the devil eat the cat.*

Go raibh páiste gach bliain agat.
*May you have a child every year.*

I dtosach na h-aicíde is fusa í a leigheas.
*It is easier to cure a disease if caught early.*

I gliobach í an chearc go dtógann sí a hál.
*The hen has ruffled feathers until she rears her brood.*

Inis do Mháire i gcógar é, is inseoidh Máire do phóbal é.
(Pronounced In-ish duh War-eh ih gug-ar aye, iss in-show-ig )
*Tell something to Mary in confidence and she will tell the whole parish.*

Is ait an mac an saol.
(Pronounced Iss att on moc an say-ol.)
*Life is strange.*

Is beo duine gan a chairde ach ní beo duine gan a phíopa.
*One may live without one's friends, but not without one's pipe.*

Is binn béal ina thost.
(Pronounced Iss bin bayl in-ah hust)
*It's a sweet mouth that is quiet. Silence is golden.*

Is buaine port ná glór na n-éan, Is buaine focal ná toice an tsaoil.
*A tune is more lasting than the song of the birds, And a word more lasting than the wealth of the world.*

Is ceirín do gach créacht an fhoighne.
*Patience is a poultice for all wounds.*

Is crua a cheannaíonn an droim an bolg.
*The back must slave to feed the belly.*

Is cuma le fear na mbróg cá leagann sé a chos.
*The man with the boots does not mind where he places his foot.*

Is cuma leis an óige cá leagann sí a cos.
*Youth does not mind where it sets its foot.*

Is é buille an phinn an buille is fealltaí.
*The pen's blow is the most treacherous.  The pen is mightier than the
sword.*

Is é do mhac do mhac go bpósann sé ach is í d'iníon go bhfaighidh
tú bás.
*Your son is your son until he marries, but your daughter is your
daughter until you die.*

Is fada an bóthar nach mbíonn casadh ann.
(Pronounced Iss faw-dah on boh-har noch(k) me-on caw-sah ann)
*It's a long road that has no turning.  Things never go completely
smoothly or badly.*

Is fearr a bheith ag lorg bídh ná a bheith ag lorg goile.
*It is better to be looking for food than to looking for an appetite.  Better to
be hungry than too sick too eat.*

Is fearr a bheith beagán sprionlaithe ná mórán caillte.
*It is better to be a little miserly than to lose a lot.*

Is fearr a bheith díomhaoin ná droch-ghnóthach.
*Better to be idle than up to no good.*

Is fearr an t-imreas ná an t-uaigneas.
*Arguing is better than loneliness.*

Is fearr an tsláinte ná na táinte.
(Pronounced Iss fahr an tlawn-teh naw na tawn-teh)
*Health is better than wealth.*

Is fearr bothán biamhar ná caisleán gortach.
*A cabin with plenty of food is better than a hungry castle.*

Is fearr cara sa chúirt ná punt sa sparán.
*A friend in court is better than a pound in the purse.*

Is fearr Gaeilge briste, ná Béarla clíste.
(Pronounced Iss faar Gay-el-geh brish-teh naw Bay-er-lah clish-teh.)
*Broken Irish is better than clever English.*

Is fearr glas ná amhras.
*A lock is better than suspicion.*

Is fearr lán doirn de cheird ná lán mála d'ór.
*A handful of skill is better than a bagful of gold.*

Is fearr lúbadh ná briseadh.
*It is better to bend than to break.*

Is fearr marcaíocht ar ghabhair ná siúlóid, dá fheabhas.
*A ride, even on a goat, is better by far than having to walk.*

Is fearr raidhse ná ganntanas.
*Plenty is better than scarcity.*

Is fearr réal inniu ná scilling amárach.
*Sixpence today is better than a shilling tomorrow; a bird in the hand is worth two in the bush.*

Is fearr rith maith ná drochsheasamh.
(Pronounced Iss fahr rih mawh naw druch(k)-hyah-sav)
*A good run is better than a bad stand. He who runs away, lives to fight another day.*

Is fearr suaimhneas ar sop ná céad bó ar chnoc.
*Peace is better than a hundred cows on a hill. The poor man can sleep soundly because he has nothing to lose.*

Is folamh fuar é teach gan bean.
*A house without a woman is empty and cold.*

Is gaire cabhair Dé ná an doras.
*God's help is nearer than the door.*

Is gaire do bhean leithscéal ná a naprún.
*An excuse is nearer to a woman than her apron.*

Is gairid ár gcairt ar an saol seo.
*Our lease on life is short.*

Is geal leis an bhfiach dubh a ghearrcach féin.
*The black raven thinks its own offspring is bright.*

Is giorra cabhair Dé ná an doras.
(Pronounced Iss gyur-rah cow-er Day naw an dur-ass)
*God's help is nearer than the door; you only have to ask for it.*

Is glas na cnoic i bhfad uainn.
*Distant hills look green.*

Is í an dias is troime is ísle a chromas a ceann.
*It is the heaviest ear of grain that bends its head the lowest.*

Is iad na muca ciúine a itheann an mhin.
*It's the quiet pig that eats the grain.*

Is in ithe na putóige atá an chruthú.
*The proof of the pudding is in the eating.*

Is maith an bhean í ach níor bhain sí a broga di go foill.
*She is a good wife, but she has not taken off her shoes yet.*

Is maith an scáthán súil charad.
*A friend's eye is a good mirror.*

Is maith an scéalaí an aimsir.
*Time is a great storyteller.*

Is maith an t-anlann an t-ocras.
(Pronounced Iss maw on tan-lan on tuc-rass)
*Hunger is a good sauce. When you're hungry, you'll eat anything!*

Is maith an t-iománaí an té a bhíonn ar an gclaí.
*The hurler on the ditch is a great fellow.*

Is milis dá ól é ach is searbh dá íoc é.
*It is sweet to drink but bitter to pay for.*

Is minic a bhain dealg beag braon.
*It is often a small thorn drew blood.*

Is minic a bheir dall ar ghiorria.
*It is often a blind person caught a hare.*

Is minic a bhíonn ciúin ciontach.
*The one who says nothing is often guilty.*

Is minic a bhris béal duine a shrón.
(Pronounced Iss min-ick a vrish bay-al din-eh a hrone.)
*Many a time a man's mouth broke his nose.*

Is minic a chealg briathra míne cailín críonna.
*Many a prudent girl was led astray with sweet words.*

Is minic a ghearr teanga duine a scornach.
*It is often a person's tongue cut his throat.*

Is minic a rinne bromach gioblach capall
(Pronounced Iss min-ick ah rin-neh brum-ach(k) cah-pawl kum-oss-ach(k))
*A ragged colt often made a powerful horse.*

Is minic cuma aingeal ar an Diabhal féin.
*There's often the look of an angel on the devil himself.*

Is namhaid í an cheird gan í a fhoghlaim.
*A craft is an enemy if not learned. You need to know what you are doing.*

Is olc an chearc nach scríobann di féin.
*It is a bad hen that does not scratch for itself.*

Is olc an ghaoth nach séideann do dhuine éigin.
(Pronounced Is ulk an gway noch(k) shay-dan do gwin-eh aye-gan.)
*It is a bad wind that does not blow to somebody. No matter how bad something that happens, someone will benefit.*

Is onórai poll ná paiste.
*A hole is more honourable than a patch.*

Is teann gach madra gearr i ndoras a thí féin.
*Every terrier is bold in the door of its house.*

Is teann madra ar a thairseacht féin.
*Every dog is bold on its own doorstep.*

Is treise an dúchas ná an oiliúint.
(Pronounced Iss tre-shah on doo-ch(k)ass naw an ill-oonch)
*Nature is stronger than nurture.*

Is treise gliocas ná neart.
*Cunning is more powerful than strength.*

Is trom an t-ualach an leisce.
*Laziness is a heavy burden.*

Is túisce deoch ná scéal.
*A drink precedes a story.*

Is uaigneach an níochán nach mbíonn léine ann.
*It is a lonely washing that has no man's shirt in it.*

Má tá moladh uait, faigh bás;  má tá cáineadh uait, pós.
*If you want praise, die; if you want complaints, marry.*

Má tá tú ag lorg cara gan locht, béidh tú gan cara go deo.
(Pronounced Maw taw too egg lor-ig kaw-rah gan luch(k), beg too gon kaw-rah guh jo)
*If you're looking for a friend without a fault, you will be without a friend forever.*

Má tá tú chun pósadh, pós anuraidh.
*If you are going to marry, marry last year.*

Mac antsaoir ábhar an tuata.
*A craftsman's son may grow up in ignorance of his father's skills.*

Mair, a chapaill, agus gheobhaidh tú féar.
*Live, horse, and you will get grass.*

Maireann an chraobh ar an bhfál ach ní mhaireann an lámh do chuir.
(Pronounced Mir-enn on ch(k)ray-ov er on vol och(k) nee mwir-enn on lawve duh ch(k)wir)
*The branch lives on the hedge but the hand that planted it be dead.*

Maireann croí éadrom i bhfad.
*A light heart lives long.*

Maireann lá go ruaig ach maireann an grá go huaigh.
*A day lasts until it's chased away but love lasts until the grave.*

Mairg nach ndéanann comhairle dea-mhná.
*Woe to him who does not have the counsel of a good wife.*

Más mian leat cáineadh pós, Más mian leat moladh faigh bás.
*If it's abuse you want, marry. If it's praise you want, die.*

Meileann muilte Dé go mall ach meileann siad go mín.
*The mills of God grind slowly but they grind finely.*

Mol an óige agus tiocfaidh sí.
(Pronounced Mull on owe-geh og-uss chuck-hig she)
*Praise youthfulness and it will respond to you. Encourage young people and they will get there.*

Molann an obair an fear.
*The work praises the man.*

Mórán cainte ar bheagán cúise.
*Much talk with little reason.*

Múineann gá seift.
*Need teaches a plan.*

Muna bhfuil agat ach pocán gabhair, bí i lár an aonaigh leis.
*If you only have a buck-goat, be in the middle of the fair with it.*

Mura gcuirfidh tú san earrach ní bhainfidh tú san fhómhar.
*If you do not sow in the spring, you will not reap in the autumn.*

Ná bí beag ná mór leis an chléir.
*Be neither unfriendly nor friendly with clergy.*

Ná bíodh do theanga faoi do chrios.
*Don't keep your tongue under your belt. Say what you want to say.*

Na ceithre rud is measa amú;ceann tinn, béal seirbh, intinn
bhuartha, agus poca folamh.
*The four least useful things; a headache, a bitter mouth, a worried mind,
and an empty pocket.*

Ná feic a bhfeicir, Is ná clois a gcloisir.Is má fiafraítear díot, Abair
ná feadrais.
*Don't see what you see, Don't hear what you hear.And if you're asked,
Say you don't know.*

Ná gabh bean gan locht.
*Do not take a wife without fault.*

Ná glac duine choíche ar a thuaraisc fhéin.
*Never accept anyone's own opinion of themselves.*

Ná lagadh Dia do lámh.
(Pronounced Naw la-gah Dee-ah duh lawve)
*May God never weaken your hand when someone has done you a*
*kindness or a favor.*

Ná leathnaigh do bhrat muna féidir leat á chosaint.
*Don't unfurl your flag if you are unable to defend it.*

Ná nocht d'fhiacla go bhféadair an greim do bhreith.
*Don't bare your teeth until you can bite.*

Ná pós bean gan locht (mar níl a leithéid ann !)
*Don't marry your ideal woman (because there is no such thing!)*

Ní bhíonn an rath ach mar a mbíonn an smacht.
(Pronounced Nee vee-on on rah och(k) mor a mee-on on smockt)
*Theres' no prosperity without discipline/control.*

Ni bhíonn cuimhne ar an arán a hitear.
*There is no recollection of eaten bread. Eaten bread is soon forgotten.*

Ní chaitheann an chaint an t-éadach.
*Talk doesn't wear the clothes.*
Ní dhéanfadh an saol capall rása d'asal.
(Pronounced Nee yane-hog on say-ol kop-al raw-sah dih-aw-sal)
*Nobody can make a racehorse out of a donkey.=You can't make a silk*
*purse out of a sow's ear*

Ní féasta go rósta, 'is ní céasta go pósta.
*There is no feast like a roast, and no torment like a marriage.*

Ní féasta go rósta, ní céasadh go pósta.
*There is no feast without a roast, there is no torment without being married.*

Ní heaspa do díth carad.
*There is no need like the lack of a friend.*

Ní heolas go haontíos.
(Pronounced Nee ho-lass guh hay-on-tee-os)
*You must live with a person to know a person.*

Ní huasal ná íseal, ach thuas seal is thíos seal.
(Pronounced Nee hoo-sal naw ee-shal, och(k) shal iss he-oss shal)
*Neither noble nor lowly, but up for a while and down for a while. It doesn't matter who you are, you will have your ups and downs.*

Ní lia duine ná barúil.
(Pronounced Nee lee-ah din-eh naw bah-rule)
*There are as many people as opinions. There'll always be disagreements.*

Ní mar a síltear a bítear.
*Things may not be as they seem to be.*

Ní mhaireann rith maith ag an each i gcónaí.
(Pronounced Nee wir-enn rih mah egg an ahch(k) ih go-nee)
*The steed does not keep his speed forever.*

Ní neart go cur le chéile.
(Pronounced Nee nyart guh cur le ch(k)aye-leh .)
*There's strength in unity.*

Ní ólann na mná leann ach imíonn sé lena linn.
*Women do not drink liquor but it disappears when they are present.*

Ní scéal rúin é ó tá a fhios ag triúr é.
*It is not a secret after three people know it.*

Ní thagann ciall roimh aois.
(Pronounced Nee hog-ann kee-al riv eesh)
*Sense comes with age.*

Ní théann na paidreacha agus na headraí le chéile.
*Prayers and idle chatter don't mix.*

Ní thuigeann an sách an seang.
(Pronounced Nee hig-ann on sawch(k) on shang)
*The well-fed does not understand the lean.*

Ní thuirsítear fear na héadála.
*One does not tire of a profitable occupation.*

Ní túisce craiceann na seanchaorach ar an bhfraigh ná craiceann
na caorach óige.
*The skin of the old sheep is on the rafter no sooner than the skin of the
young sheep.*

Níl a fhios ag aon duine cá bhfuil fód a bháis.
*Nobody knows where his sod of death is.*

Níl aon leigheas ar an ngrá ach pósadh.
(Pronounced Neel ane lie-ass er on nraw awch(k) poe-sah)
*There's no cure for love except to marry.*

Níl aon suáilce gan a duáilce féin.
*There are no unmixed blessings in life.*

Níl aon tinteán mar do thinteán féin.
(Pronounced Neel ane tin-tawn mor duh hin-tawn fayne. )
*There's no fireplace like your own fireplace. There's no place like home.*

Níl aon tóin tinn mar do thóin tinn féin.
(Pronounced Neel ane tone-tine mor duh hone-tine fayne.)
*There's no sore ass like your own sore ass.*

Níl leigheas ar an ngrá ach pósadh.
*There is no cure for love other than marriage.*

Níl luibh ná leigheas in aghaidh an bháis.
(Pronounced Neel luv naw lie-iss in igue on vawsh)
*There is no remedy or cure against death.*

Níl ní níos géire ná teanga mná.
*There's nothing sharper than a woman's tongue.*

Níl saoi gan locht.
(Pronounced Neel see gon luch(k)t )
*There's not a wise man without fault; We have all got our weaknesses.*

Níor bhris focal maith fiacal riamh.
(Pronounced Neer vrish fuck-al maw fee-kal reeve)
*A good word never broke a tooth. A kind or encouraging word never did any harm.*

Nollaig bhreá a dhéanann reilig teann.
*A fat Christmas makes for a tight graveyard.*

Nuair a bheidh do lámh i mbéal na con tarraing go réidh í.
*When your hand is in the hound's mouth withdraw it gently.*

Nuair a bhíonn an bolg lán is mian leis na gcnáimh síneadh.
*When the stomach is full, the bones like to stretch.*

Nuair a bhíonn an cat amuigh, bíonn an luch ag rince.
*When the cat's away, the mice will play.*

Nuair a bhíonn an fíon istigh, bíonn an ciall amuigh.
(Pronounced Nuh-ar a vee-on fee-on iss-chih, vee-on an keel am-wih)
*When the wine is in, sense is out. There's no sense to someone who's drunk.*

Nuair a bhíos an braon istigh bíonn an chiall amuigh.
*When the drop is inside the sense is outside.*

Nuair is gann é an bia is ea is fial é a roinnt.
*When food is scarce it is generous to share it.*

Obair ó chrích obair bean tí.
*Work without end is housewife's work.*

Ón lá a bpósfaidh tú beidh do chroí i do bhéal agus do lámh i do phóca.
*From the day you marry your heart will be in your mouth and your hand in your pocket.*

Pós bean aniar agus pósfaidh tú thiar.
*Marry a woman from the west and you marry the west.*

Pós bean oileáin agus pósfaidh tú an t-oileán ar fad.
*Marry an island woman and you marry the whole island.*

Pós bean ón sliabh agus pósfaidh tú an sliabh ar fad.
*Marry a woman from the mountain and you will marry the entire mountain.*

San áit ina mbíonn toit bíonn tine,
San áit ina mbíonn tine bíonn teas,
San áit ina mbíonn teas bíonn mná,
San áit ina mbíonn mná bíonn gab!
*Where there's a roof, there's a fire,*
*where there's a fire, there's heat,*
*where there's heat there's women ,*
*where there's women, there's gossip!*

Seachain teach an tabhairne nó is bairnigh is beatha duit.
*Beware of the public house or limpets will be your food.*

Seachain tigh an tabhairne nó is bairnigh is beatha duit.
*Beware of the drinking house or you'll be living on barnacles.*

Síleann do chara agus do namhad nach bhfaighidh tú bás choíche.
(Pronounced Sheel-an duh ch(k)awr-ah ogg-uss duh now-ad nawch(k) vy-ig too bawss ch(k)wee-ch(k)eh)
*Both your friend and your enemy thing that you will never die.*

Sliocht sleachta ar sliocht bhur sleachta!
*May you have children and your children have children.*

Snathán fada, táilliur falsa.
*A long stitch, a lazy tailor.*

Súil le cúiteamh a mhilleas an cearrbhach.
(Pronounced Su-ell leh koo-it-av ah vill-ass on ky-ar-vaw-ch)
*Hoping to recoup is what ruins the card player.*

Tá onóir ag an aois agus uaisle ag an óige
(Pronounced Tah on-ower egg on eesh ogg-uss ush-le egg on owe-egg-eh)
*Age is honorable and youth is noble.*

Tá trí shaghas bean ann: bean chomh mí-náireach le muc, bean chomh crosta le cearc agus bean chomh mín leis an uan.
*There are three kinds of women: a women as shameless as a pig, a woman as contrary as a hen and a women as gentle as a lamb.*

Thuillfeadh éinne airgead, ach is fear gasta a choiméadfadh é.
*Anyone would earn money, but it is a clever man who would hold on to it.*

Tosach sláinte codladh.
*Sleep is the first sign of recovery.*

Trí ní is deacair a thuiscint; intleacht na mban, obair na mbeach, teacht agus imeacht na taoide.
*Three things that are difficult to understand; the mind of a woman, the work of bees and the coming and going of the tide.*

Triúr fear go dteipeann orthu mná a thuiscint: fír óga, fir aosta agus fir mhéanaosta.
*Three kinds of men who fail to understand women: young men, old men and middle-aged men.*

Tuigeann Tadhg Taidhgín.
*Like understands like.*

Tús maith leath na hoibre.
(Pronounced Toose mawh lah na hib-reh)
*A good start is half the work.*

Tús na heagna eagla an Tiarna.
*Wisdom begins with the fear of the Lord.*

# 6 Celtic Proverbs in English

A bad trade is better than idleness.

A bad workman quarrels with his tools.

A big church yields small devotions.

A blanket is better off being doubled.

A buckle is a fine addition to an old shoe.

A cat can look at a king.

A chance shot may kill the devil.

A child desires what fills his eye.

A closed fist never caught a bird.

A combed head sells the feet.

A dead hen is done laying.

A drink precedes a story.

A farmer's work is never done.

A flying bird is any man's shot.

A friend's eye is a good mirror.

A full cabin is better than an empty castle.

A glowing gríosach (ember) is easily rekindled.

A golden ring can tie a man as tight as any chain.

A good coat covers a lot of rags.

A good denial — the best point in law.

A good eye is worth two pairs of hands.

A good farmer is known by his crops.

A good friend in court is better than money in the purse.

A good laugh and a long sleep are the two best cures.

A good retreat is better than a bad stand.

A good turn in the kitchen is as good as a prayer in the chapel.

A good word never broke a tooth.

A grain often came whole from the grinding.

A greyhound finds its food in its feet.

A growing moon and a flowing tide are lucky times to marry.

A handstaff of holly, a buailtin of hazel, a single sheaf, and a clean floor.

A heavy purse makes a light heart.

A hen is heavy when carried far.

A hound's food is in its legs.

A law is costly; better to shake hands and be friends.

A lawmaker is a law-breaker.

A lawyer's house is made of fools' heads.

A lie looks the better of having a witness.

A life making mistakes is not only more honorable, but more useful than a life spent doing nothing at all.

A little dog can start a hare, but it takes a big one to catch it.

A little fire to warm you is better than a great one to harm you.

A lock is better than suspicion.

A lucky person needs only to be born.

A man cannot grow rich without his wife's leave.

A man cannot grow rich without his wife's leave.

A man is shy in another man's corner.

A man may live after losing his life but not after losing his honor.

A man never fails among his own people.

A man takes a drink, the drink takes a drink, the drink takes the man.

A man takes a drink, the drink takes a drink, the drink takes the man.

A man without dinner — two for supper.

A man's best friend is his mother until he meets his wife.

A masterless dog will travel far.

A meeting in the sunlight is lucky, as is a burying in the rain.

A narrow neck keeps the bottle from being emptied in one swig.

A nod is as good as a wink to a blind horse.

A nod is as good as a wink to the blind horse.

A poem ought to be well made at first, for there is many a one to spoil it afterwards.

A rambling bee brings home the honey.

A Sabbath well-spent brings a week of content.

A scholar's ink lasts longer than a martyr's blood.

A short visit is best and that not too often.

A sick man reported dead always recovers.

A sign of an old law is an old song.

A silent mouth is melodious.

A silent mouth is sweet to hear.

A slow hound is often lucky.

A sly rogue is often in good dress.

A smokey cabin, a handful of spuds, and a flea-filled bed.

A soft dropping April brings milk to cows and sheep.

A spark may raise an awful blaze.

A trade not properly learned is an enemy.

A trout in the ashes is better than a salmon in the water.

A tune is more lasting than the song of birds, and a word more lasting than the wealth of the world.

A wedge from itself splits the oak tree.

A wet day is a good day for changing a pound.

A whistling woman and a crowing hen will bring no luck to the house they are in.

A windy day is not the day for thatching.

A wise man never saw a dead man walk.

A woman can beat the devil.

Accept gifts with a sigh; most men give to be paid.

Age is honorable and youth is noble.

All are not saints that go to church.

All good has an end save the goodness of God.

All is grist that comes to the mill.

All the world's a stage and most of us are desperately unrehearsed.

All wealth is consumed by small spending.

Always remember that hindsight is the best insight to foresight.

An empty barn needs no roof.

An empty house needs no thatch.

An Irishman after trying American beer for the first time: "Put it back in the horse!"

An Irishman is never at peace except when he's fighting.

An oak is often split by a wedge from its own branch.

An old broom knows the dirty corners best.

An old dog cannot alter his way of barking.

Any Kerryman will tell you that there are only two Kingdoms: the Kingdom of God and the Kingdom of Kerry - One is not of this world and the other is out of this world.

Any man can lose his hat in a fairy wind.

Any man who owns a cow can always find a woman to milk her.

Apples will grow again.

As honest as a cat when the meat is out of reach.

As the big hound is, so will the pup be.

As the old cock crows, the young cock learns.

As you live yourself you judge your neighbor.

As you slide down the banister of life, may the splinters never point in the wrong direction.

As you slide down the banister of life, may the splinters never point the wrong way.

Autumn days come quickly like the running of a hound on the moor.

Bad goods never yet went to the market that some blind market-man did not buy.

Bad luck never comes its lone.

Bare is the companionless shoulder.

Bareness is better than misfortune.

Be kind to those that meet you as you rise; you may pass them again as you fall.

Be neither intimate nor distant with the clergy.

Be the road straight or crooked, the high road is the shortest.

Beauty does not make the pot boil.

Beauty is only skin deep; ugliness goes to the bone.

Beauty won't make the kettle boil.

Before answering a question, an Irishman always asks one.

Bend with the tree that will bend with you.

Better an idle house than a bad tenant.

Better be sparing at first than at last.

Better fifty enemies outside the house than one within.

Better for a man to have even a dog welcome him than a dog bark at him.

Better good manners than good looks.

Better is a small fish than an empty dish.

Better is the small fire that warms on the little day of peace than the big fire that burns on the great day of wrath.

Better old debts than old grudges.

Better the devil you know than the devil you don't know.

Better the trouble that follows death than the trouble that follows shame.

Better to be a man of character than a man of means.

Better to be fortunate than rich.

Better to be lucky than wise.

Blow not on dead embers.

Both your friend and your enemy think you will never die.

Bravery is not lasting.

Burning embers are easily kindled.

Call no man a wise man until the worms have done with him.

Choose your company before you drink.

Clean and whole make poor clothes shine.

Constant company wears out its welcome.

Consult your purse before you buy.

Court abroad but marry at home.

Credit to harvest and credit forever.

Cut your coat according to your cloth.

Dead men tell no tales but there's many a thing learned in the wake-house.

Death does not take a bribe.

Death is the master of the world.

Death is the poor man's doctor.

Death puts its own appearance on everyone.

Do not bless the fish until it is landed.

Do not burn your fingers when you have tongs.

Do not buy a purse with your last half-crown.

Do not resent growing old.  Many are denied the privilege.

Do not throw away old boots until you get new ones.

Don't be hard and don't be soft and don't desert your friend for your own share.

Don't be too friendly with the clergy and don't fall out with them.

Don't bid the devil good day till you meet him.

Don't break your shins on your neighbor's pots.

Don't desert the highway for the shortcut.

Don't go to law with the devil in the court of hell.

Don't make bold with the sea.

Don't make little of your dish for it may be an ignorant fellow who judges it.

Don't pluck the goose until you catch her.

Don't show your skin to a person who won't cover it.

Don't show your skin to a person who won't cover it.

Don't skin the deer until you catch it.

Don't take a slate off your own house to put on your neighbor's.

Don't tell secrets to the children of your relatives.

Don't run for the priest after the patient has died.

Drink a pint in memory of a friend, then let the dead rest in peace.

Drink is the curse of the land: it makes you fight your neighbor, it makes you shoot at your landlord, and it makes you miss him.

Drinking gives one a very clear sense of who's to blame for everything.

Drunkenness and anger speak the truth.

Earth has no sorrows that heaven cannot heal.

Earth has no sorrows that heaven cannot heal.

Enough and no waste is as good as a feast.

Even a small thorn causes festering.

Even a tin knocker will shine on a dirty door.

Even a tin knocker will shine on a dirty door.

Every branch blossoms according to the root from which it sprung.

Every branch blossoms according to the root from which it sprung.

Every cat is grey at night.

Every dog is brave on his own doorstep.

Every finger has not the same length, nor every son the same disposition.

Every hound is a pup until he hunts.

Every man is sociable until a cow invades his garden.

Every man's mind is his kingdom.

Every mother thinks it's for her own child the sun rises.

Everyone feels his own wound first.

Everyone is nice until the cow gets into the garden.

Everyone is sweet to your face until you burn a sack of turf with them.

Everyone lays a burden on the willing horse.

Everything troubles you and the cat breaks your heart.

Experience is the comb that life gives a bald man.

Faith is better than fasting, and love crowns both.

Faithful are the wounds of a friend, but an enemy's kisses are deceitful.

Firelight will not let you read fine stories but its warm and you won't see the dust on the floor.

First catch the hare and then cook it.

Forgetting a debt doesn't mean it's paid.

Fortune is a thing worth searching for.

Friends are better than gold.

Friends are like fiddle-strings — they must not be screwed too tightly.

Friendship is a fine thing though bitter is the parting.

Friendship will not stand on one leg.

Give to the child and it will visit you again.

God fits the back to suit the burden.

God invented whiskey to keep the Irish from ruling the world.

God is good and the devil is not bad, either.

God is good but don't dance in a church.

God is good but don't dance in a currach.

God is good to the Irish, but no one else is; not even the Irish.

God never closes one door without opening another.

God prefers prayers to tears.

God prefers prayers to tears.

God's help is nearer than the door.

Good as drink is, it ends in thirst.

Good care takes the sting off bad luck.

Good is the mill which has been worn-out.

Good luck comes in slender currents; misfortune comes in rolling torrents.

Half a leap falls into the ditch.

Handsome is as handsome does.

Have your own fire or trust to the sun for a warming.

He was a bold man that first ate an oyster.

He who can follow his own will is a king.

He who comes with a story to you brings two away from you.

He who drinks water does not get drunk.

He who gets a name for early rising can stay in bed until midday.

He who has spent a long life has many a story.

He who has water and peat on his farm has the world his own way.

He who has water and peat on his own farm has the world his own way.

He who pays the piper calls the tune.

He who stares into the middle of the fire does be heavily in love.

Heaven's leac na teine (stone before the fire) is reserved for the poor.

Heaven's stone before the fire is reserved for the poor.

Here's to a long life and a merry one. A quick death and an easy one. A pretty girl and an honest one. A cold pint and another one!

Here's to me, and here's to you. And here's to love and laughter. I'll be true as long as you. And not one moment after.

Here's to women's kisses, and to whiskey, amber clear. Not as sweet as a woman's kiss, but a darn sight more sincere!

Honey is sweet, but don't lick it off a briar.

Hope protects the oppressed.

However long the day, night must fall.

However long the road there comes a turning.

Hunger is a good sauce.

I don't consider myself a heavy drinker, I often go hours without touching a drop.

I have my faults, but changing my tune is not one of them.

I once read about the evils of drink, so I gave up reading.

I spent a lot of good money on drink, women and cars, the rest I just squandered

I'd rather have a full bottle in front of me than a full frontal lobotomy.

Idle dogs worry sheep.

If a cat had a dowry, she would often be kissed.

If children won't make you laugh, they won't make you cry.

If God sends you down a stony path, may he give you strong shoes.

If God sends you down a stony path, may he give you strong shoes.

If it's drowning you're after, don't torment yourself with shallow water.

If it's drowning you're after, don't torment yourself with shallow water.

If the cat sits long enough at the hole, she will catch the mouse.

If there is a way into the woods there is always a way out it it.

If you buy what you don't need you might have to sell what you do.

If you come up in this world be sure not to go down in the next.

If you dig a grave for others you may fall into it yourself.

If you do not sow in the spring you will not reap in the autumn.

If you don't know the way, walk slowly.

If you don't want flour on your clothes, stay out of the mill.

If you don't want flour on your shoes, don't go into the mill.

If you go to court, leave your soul at home.

If you have a roving eye, it's no use having the other one fixed on Heaven.

If you have one pair of good soles, it is better than two pairs of good uppers.

If you move old furniture it may fall to bits.

If you put a silk dress on a goat, he is still a goat.

If you want praise, die. If you want blame, marry.

If you want to be criticized, marry.

If you're enough lucky to be Irish... You're lucky enough!

If your messenger is slow, go to meet him.

In God there is no night and day.

In winter, the milk goes to the cow's horns.

Instinct is stronger than morality.

Instinct is stronger than upbringing.

Ireland is a fruitful mother of genius, but a barren nurse.

Irish Alzheimer's -you forget everything except the grudges.

Irish Diplomacy... is the ability to tell a man to go to hell so that he looks forward to making the trip.

It is a bad hen that does not scratch herself.

It is a bad hen that will not scratch herself.

It is a lonesome washing that doesn't have a man's shirt in it.

It is a long road that has no turning.

It is a poor house that can't keep one lady.

It is a rocky road to heaven.

It is as hard to see a woman crying as it is to see a barefoot duck.

It is better to be refused a hook on harvest day than to be refused for a wife.

It is better to exist unknown to the law.

It is better to spend money like there's no tomorrow than to spend tonight like there's no money!

It is easier to knock down a house than to build one.

It is easy to kindle a fire on an old hearth.

It is easy to preach to the devil with a full stomach.

It is far away what God sends.

It is for the sake of company dogs go to church.

It is hard for an empty bag to stand its lone.

It is hard to escape the bonds of love.

It is hard to put a dog off his track.

It is more difficult to maintain honor than to become prosperous.

It is no use carrying an umbrella if your shoes are leaking.

It is not a fish until it is on the bank.

It is not a secret if it is known by three people.

It is not natural to have smoke without fire, nor fire without people.

It is not the most beautiful woman who has the most sense.

It is not the same to go to the king's house as to come from it.

It is not the same to go to the king's house as to come from it.

It is often that a person's mouth broke his nose.

It is only at home that one finds relations.

It is sweet to drink but bitter to pay for.

It is the flattering harp which never lacked golden strings.

It is the fool who has luck.

It is the good horse that draws its own cart.

It is the quiet pig that eats the meal.

It is the quiet pigs that eat the meal.

It takes time to build castles. Rome wan not built in a day.

It's a bad hound that's not worth the whistling.

It's a dirty bird that won't keep its own nest clean.

It's a hard-fought battle from which no man returns to tell the tale.

It's a pure spring that never runs dry.

It's an ill wind that blows nobody good.

It's difficult to choose between two blind goats.

It's easy to halve the potato where there's love.

It's hard to kill a bad thing.

It's no use boiling your cabbage twice.

It's no use carrying an umbrella if your shoes are leaking.

It's not a delay to stop and sharpen the scythe.

It's the first drop that destroys you, there's no harm at all in the last.

It's easy to halve the potato where there's love.

It's my rule never to lose me temper till it would be detrimental to keep it.

It's not a matter of upper and lower class but of being up a while and down a while.

Its own child is bright to the carrion crow.

Keep the bone and the dog will follow you.

Keep your shop and your shop will keep you.

Lack of resource has hanged many a person.

Laziness is a heavy burden.

Let each person judge his own luck, good or bad.

Lie down with dogs and you'll rise with fleas.

Life is a strange lad.

Life is but a vapor.

Life is like a cup of tea, it's all in how you make it!

Listen to the sound of the river and you will get a trout.

Listen to the sound of the river and you'll catch a trout.

Little by little the oak tree grows.

Little possessions, little care.

Loneliness is better than bad company.

Long sleep renders a child inert.

Lose an hour in the morning and you'll be looking for it all day.

Love all men save an attorney.

Love is no impartial judge.

Luck and laziness go hand in hand.

Luck is a king and luck is a beggar.

Luck seldom lasts.

Man talks, but God directs.

Many a day shall we rest in the clay.

Many a rose-cheeked apple is rotten to the core.

Many a sudden change takes place on an unlikely day.

Many a white collar covers a dirty neck.

Many an honest heart beats under a ragged coat.

Many an Irish property was increased by the lace of a daughter's petticoat.

Many feathers make a bed.

Marriages are all happy; it's having breakfast together that causes all the problems.

Marry a mountain woman and you marry the mountain.

May misfortune follow you the rest of your life, and never catch up.

May neighbours respect you, trouble neglect you, the angels protect you, and Heaven accept you.

May the luck of the Irish be with you!

May the roof above you never fall in, and those gathered beneath it never fall out.

May you always have a clean shirt, a clear conscience, and enough coins in your pocket to buy a pint!

May you be poor in misfortune, rich in blessings, slow to make enemies and quick to make friends. And may you know nothing but happiness from this day forward.

May you die in bed at 95, shot by a jealous spouse.

May you get all your wishes but one, so that you will always have something to strive for!

May you have a bright future - as the chimney sweep said to his son.

May you have food and raiment, a soft pillow for your head. May you be forty years in heaven before the devil knows you're dead.

May you have the hindsight to know where you've been, the foresight to know where you are going, and the insight to know when you have gone too far.

May you live as long as you want and never want as long as you live.

May you live to be 100 years, with one extra year to repent.

May your heart be light and happy, may your smile be big and wide, and may your pockets always have a coin or two inside!

May your home always be too small to hold all your friends.

May your thoughts be as glad as the shamrocks. May your heart be as light as a song. May each day bring you bright, happy hours that stay with you all the year long.

Melodious is the closed mouth.

Men are like bagpipes—no sound comes from them until they're full.

Mere words do not feed the friars.

Money does not make you happy but it quiets the nerves

Money makes the horse gallop whether he has shoes or not.

More grows on a tilled field than is sowed in it.

Nature breaks through the eyes of the cat.

Nature will come through the claws, and the hound will follow the hare.

Necessity is the mother of invention.

Necessity knows no law.

Need teaches a plan.

Neither break a law nor make one.

Neither give cherries to a pig or advice to a fool.

Never be the first in the bog or last in the wood.

Never bolt your door with a boiled carrot.

Never bolt your door with a boiled carrot.

Never burn a penny candle looking for a half-penny

Never buy a rabbit without a head, as it may be a cat.

Never buy bread from a butcher.

Never buy through your ears but through your eyes.

Never cross the fields while you have the road to go.

Never dread the winter till the snow is on the blanket.

Never sell a hen on a wet day.

Never sell a hen on a wet day.

Never sleep with a stranger or borrow from a neighbor.

Never want while your neighbor has it.

New kings make new laws.

No ghost as bad as the live ghost.

No man ever wore a tie as nice as his child's arm around his neck.

No two people ever lit a fire without disagreeing.

Noiseless is the approach of the avenging deities.

None can know the truth except God.

Often a cow does not take after its breed.

Old proverbs are the children of truth.

On an unknown path, every foot is slow.

One dog can't fight.

One must pay health its tithe.

One story brings on another.

One tale is good until another is told.

One who is cowless must be his own dog.

Only a fool burns his coal without warming himself.

Only Irish coffee provides all main essential food groups: alcohol, caffeine, sugar, and fat.

Only those who were born to hang are not afraid of the water.

Out of the kitchen comes the tune.

Patience is poultice for all wounds.

People live in each other's shelter.

Perfection is something that cannot be achieved, it is something that we strive for.

Perseverance is the mother of good luck.

Pity him who makes an opinion a certainty.

Poor is the church without music.

Poor people have poor weddings.

Poverty waits at the gates of idleness.

Praise the ripe field not the green corn

Praise the ripe field not the green corn.

Praise the sea but keep near land.

Praise the young and they will make progress.

Promise is in honor's debt.

Put silk on a goat, and it's still a goat.

Questioning is the door of knowledge.

Quiet people are well able to look after themselves.

Rain is also very difficult to film, particularly in Ireland because it's quite fine, so fine that the Irish don't even acknowledge that it exists.

Riding on a goat is better than the best of walking.

Satin and silk, velvet and scarlet, often put out the kitchen fire.

Seeing is believing, but feeling is the God's own truth.

Seldom is the last of anything better than the first.

Sending for the doctor is brother to death.

Shallow brooks are noisy.

Shut your mouth and eat your dinner.

Silence is the fence around the haggard where wisdom is stacked.

Slow is every foot on an unknown path.

Snuff at a wake is fine if there is nobody sneezing at the snuff box.

Some cause happiness wherever they go; others whenever they

go.

Sometimes one day changes everything; sometimes years change nothing.

Speak to the devil and you'll hear the clatter of his hooves.

Strife is better than loneliness.

Stupidity is sending the goose on a mission to the fox's den.

Sweet the corners — the middle will sweep itself.

Take the drink for the thirst that is to come.

Taste and try before you buy.

Tea seldom spoils if water boils.

Tears bring nobody back from the grave.

Tell the truth and shame the devil.

That a poet is born, not made, is well-known.

The beauty of an old shoe is to polish it.

The best candle for man is common sense.

The best looking-glass is the eyes of a friend.

The best way to keep loyalty in a man's heart is to keep money in his purse.

The cat is always dignified, until the dog comes by.

The child that's left to himself will put his mother to shame.

The cocks crow but the hens lay the eggs.

The color of the cheek cannot disguise the feelings of the heart.

The day will come when the cow will have use for her tail.

The deed will praise itself.

The deeper the well the sweeter the water.

The devil dances in an empty pocket.

The devil is good to his own in this world, and bad to them in the next.

The dog follows the man who has the bone.

The dog that's always on the go, is better than the one that's always curled up.

The doorstep of a great house is slippery.

The eye should be blind in the house of another.

The fear of God is the beginning of wisdom.

The first drop will destroy you; there's no harm in the last.

The first story from the host, stories until dawn from the guest.

The first year is the kissing year; the second year is the fisting year.

The friend that can be bought is not worth buying.

The great Gaels of Ireland are the men that God made mad. For all their wars are merry, and all their songs are sad.

The greenest wood is fated to lose its bloom.

The habit does not make the monk.

The hole is more honorable than the patch.

The Irish are a very fair people, they never speak well of one another.

The Irish forgive their great men when they are safely buried.

The Irish gave the bagpipes to the Scots as a joke, but the Scots haven't seen the joke yet.

The law of heredity runs through the cat's eyes.

The life of an old hat is to cock it.

The light heart lives long.

The longest road has an end and the straightest road has an end.

The longest road out is the shortest road home.

The longest road out is the shortest road home.

The love of God guides every good.

The lucky man waits for prosperity; the unfortunate man takes a leap in the dark.

The man who pays the piper calls the tune.

The man who sees what he loves knows true happiness.

The man with a cow doesn't need a scythe.

The man with a cow doesn't need a scythe.

The man with the boots does not mind where he places his foot.

The memory of an old child is long.

The mill cannot grind with the water that has passed.

The mill that grinds must have water.

The mills of God grind slowly but they grind finely.

The mills of the gods grind slowly but they grind finely.

The minister christens his own child first.

The moon is none the worse for having the dogs bark at her.

The morning of the race is not the morning to feed your horse.

The mouth of the grave gives to the needy one.

The nearer the church the further from God.

The newest food and the oldest of drink!

The old dog for the hard road and leave the pup on the path.

The old pipe gives the sweetest smoke.

The older the buck, the harder the horn.

The older the fiddle the sweeter the tune.

The older the fiddle, the sweeter the tune.

The oldest man that ever lived died at last.

The peacemaker does not go free.

The people come and go, but the hills remain.

The person bringing good news knocks boldly on the door.

The pig in the sty doesn't know the pig going along the road.

The race of the hound through the bog is the harvest of night falling.

The raggity colt often makes a powerful horse.

The reason the Irish are always fighting each other iIs they have no other worthy opponents.

The river is no wider from this side than the other.

The river is no wider from this side than the other.

The road to Heaven is well signposted, but it is badly lit at night.

The road to Heaven is well signposted, but it is badly lit at night.

The road to hell is paved with good intentions.

The schoolhouse bell sounds bitter in youth and sweet in old age.

The seed you sow is the corn you will reap.

The shelter of the bush is not noticed until it is gone.

The shoemaker's horses and the blacksmith's horses often go unshod.

The slow horse reaches the mill.

The smaller the cabin the wider the door.

The smallest thing outlives the human being.

The swiftness of the roe is known without loosing the hounds.

The taste of the clover makes a thief of the dove.

The thing that is bought dear is often sold cheap.

The three best friends and the three worst enemies: fire, wind, and water.

The three faults of drinking are: a sorrowful morning, a dirty coat, and an empty pocket.

The three kinds of people who will get to heaven quickest after death: a young child after baptism, a young priest after ordination, and a tiller of the soil.

The three most nourishing foods: beef marrow, the meat of a chicken, and Guinness Stout.

The three sweetest sounds: the sound of the quern, the lowing of the cow, the cry of a child.

The wealth of heaven lasts forever.

The wearer best knows where the shoe pinches.

The well fed does not understand the lean.

The wisdom of the proverb cannot be surpassed.

The wise bird flies the lowest.

The wood will renew the foliage it sheds.

The work praises the man.

The world would not make a racehorse of a donkey.

The world's a stage and most of us are desperately unrehearsed

There are finer fish in the sea than have ever been caught.

There are fish in the sea better than have ever been caught.

There are no trials until one gets married.

There are only three kinds of Irish men who can't understand women— young men, old men, and men of middle age.

There are only two kinds of people in the world, the Irish and those who wish they were.

There are two things that cannot be cured: death and the want of sense.

There is a crock of gold in the tomb of every chieftain, but they are all guarded by cats and fairies.

There is hope from the sea, but none from the grave.

There is luck in leisure.

There is luck in sharing a thing.

There is more friendship in a jigger of whiskey than in a churn of buttermilk.

There is never an old brogue but there's a foot to fit it.

There is no anguish of soul until one has children.

There is no cure for love but marriage.

There is no fireside like your own fireside.

There is no luck except where there is discipline.

There is no luck except where there is discipline.

There is no need like the lack of a friend.

There is no overtaking the shot once fired.

There is no strength without unity.

There is no such thing as bad publicity except your own obituary.

There is no use in shouting at the fair when you have nothing to sell.

There is no worse want than the want of fire.

There is nothing in the world so poor as going to hell.

There is only one thing worse than being talked about, and that is not being talked about.

There is pain in prohibition.

There is work for the mill when the harrow works.

There never came a gatherer but a scatterer came after him.

There never was an old slipper but there was an old stocking to match it.

There was never a scabby sheep in a flock that didn't like to have a comrade.

There was never yet a wood but contained its own burning.

There'll be white blackbirds before an unwilling woman ties the knot.

There's favor in hell and the biggest devil gets it.

There's little value in the single cow.

There's many a good tune played on an old fiddle.

There's neither success nor efficiency without authority and laws.

There's no better judge than the battlefield.

There's no crime in the blow that has not been struck.

There's no forcing the sea.

There's no love until there's family.

There's no need to fear the wind if your haystacks are tied down.

There's no point in keeping a dog if you are going to do your own barking.

There's no point in keeping a dog if you are going to do your own barking.

There's nothing so bad that it couldn't be worse.

There's no reason to bring religion into it. I think we ought to have as great a regard for religion as we can, so as to keep it out of as many things as possible.

They are scarce of news that speak ill of their mother.

Thirst is the end of drinking and sorrow is the end of drunkenness.

Thirst is the end of drinking and sorrow is the end of love.

Those who drink to forget, please pay in advance

Though the old proverb may be given up, it is nonetheless true.

Threatened dogs live long.

Three candles that illuminate every darkness: truth, nature, knowledge.

Three chains by which evil propensity is bound: a covenant, a monastic rule, law.

Three clouds that obscure the sight of wisdom: forgetfulness, ignorance, and a little knowledge.

Three dead ones that are paid for with living things: an apple-tree,a hazel bush,a sacred grove.

Three diseases without shame: Love, itch and thirst.

Three feasts due to everyone: the feast of baptism, the feast of marriage, and the feast of death.

Three keys that unlock the secrets of the soul: heavy drinking, violent temper, and innocent trust.

Three men who are difficult to talk to: a king about his booty, a Viking in his hauberk, a boor who's under patronage.

Three pairs that never agree: two married women in the same house, two cats with one mouse, and two bachelors courting the same woman.

Three sources of new life: a woman's stomach, a hen's egg, and a wrong forgiven.

Three things every chieftain needs: justice, peace, and an army.

Three things that a man should never be without: a cat, a chimney, and a woman of the house.

Three things that are always cold: a dog's nose, a man's elbow, and a maid's knee.

Three things that are difficult to understand; the mind of a woman, the work of bees, and the coming and going of the tide.

Three things that cannot be taught: a singing voice, generosity, and poetry.

Three things that run swiftest: a stream of fire, a stream of water, and a stream of falsehood.

Three things that stay longest in a family: fighting, drinking, and red hair.

Three things you cannot comprehend are: the mind of a woman, the working of the bees, and the ebb and flow of the tide.

Three things you cannot comprehend: the mind of a woman, the working of bees, and the ebb and flow of the tide.

Three types of men who fail to understand women: young men, old men, and middle-aged men.

Three types of men who fail to understand women: young men, old men, and middle-aged men.

Three worst smiles: the smile of a wave, the smile of a loose woman, the grin of a dog ready to leap.

Time and patience would bring a snail to America.

Time is a good storyteller.

Time is a great story teller.

Time used sharpening a scythe is not time wasted.

To please herself only does the cat purr.

Too many cats are worse than rats.

True is every proverb, false every superstition.

Truth is bitter, but never shamed.

Twenty years a child; twenty years running wild; twenty years a mature man; and after that, praying.

Two people never lit a fire without disagreeing.

Two shorten the road.

Two shortens the road.

Two thirds of the work is the semblance.

Unwillingness easily finds an excuse.

Walk straight, my son - as the old crab said to the young crab.

Water is a good drink if taken in the right spirit.

What butter and whiskey won't cure, there's no cure for.

What everybody says must be true.

What I am afraid to hear I'd better say first myself.

What is nearest the heart is nearest the lips.

What should you expect from a cat but a kitten?

What the child sees, the child does. What the child does, the child is.

What would a cat's son do but kill a rat?

What's the use of being Irish if the world doesn't break your heart?

When a heifer is far from home she grows longer horns.

When a heifer is far from home she grows longer horns.

When a twig grows hard it is difficult to twist it. Every beginning is weak.

When all fruits fail welcome haws.

When fire is applied to a stone it cracks.

When luck comes, it comes by the bucketful.

When the apple is ripe it will fall.

When the apple is ripe it will fall.

When the drop (drink) is inside, the sense is outside.

When the liquor was gone the fun was gone.

When the liquor was gone the fun was gone.

When the two ends are alight the candle does not burn long.

When you're not fishing be mending the nets.

When your hand is in the dog's mouth, withdraw it gently.

Where the tongue slips, it speaks the truth.

Whiskey when you're sick makes you well; whiskey when you're well makes you sick.

Who brings a tale takes two away.

Who gossips to you will gossip of you.

Who gossips with you will gossip of you.

Who keeps his tongue keeps his friends.

Wide is the door of the little cottage.

Willows are weak, but they will bind other wood.

Wine divulges truth.

Wine drowns more men than water.

Wine is better than blood.

Wine is old men's milk.

Wine is sweet but the results are bitter.

Wine makes old women wenches.

Woe to him who does not heed a good wife's counsel.

Woe to him whose betrayer sits at his table.

Woe to the person who rears not a child of his own.

Women do not drink liquor but it disappears when they are present.

Work is better than talk.

You can't expect a big egg from a little hen.

You can't sell the cow and drink her milk.

You cannot have the hen and the price of her.

You cannot make a silk purse out of a sow's ear.

You know it's summer in Ireland when the rain gets warmer.

You may as well give cherries to a pig as advice to a fool.

You must live with a person to know a person. If you want to know me come and live with me.

You must summer and winter a stranger before you can form an opinion of him.

You must take the little potato with the big potato.

You never know the want of water until the well has gone dry.

You never miss the water till the well runs dry.

You won't learn to swim on the kitchen floor.

You'll never plough a field by turning it over in your mind.

You'll never plow a field by turning it over in your mind.

You've got to do your own growing, no matter how tall your grandfather was.

Young people don't know what old age is, and old people forget what youth was.

Your son is your son until he takes a wife, but your daughter is your daughter all your life.

Youth does not mind where it sets its foot.

Youth likes to wander.

You've got to do your own growing, no matter how tall your father was.

You've got to do your own growing, no matter how tall your grandfather was.

# 7 Celtic Proverbs in "Old West Highlander"

A bairn must creep ere he gang.

A begun work is half ended.

A bettlesie brain cannot lye.

A black shoe makes a blythe heart.

A bleat Cat makes a proud Mouse.

A blind man should not judge of colours.

A blyth heart makes a blomand visage.

A borrowed len should come laughing ahme.

A broken a Ship hes come to land.

A burnt bairn fire dreads.

A Cock is crouse upon his own midding.

A cumbersome Cur in company is hated for his miscarriage.

A dum man holds all.

A dum man wan never land.

A Fair Bride is soon buskt, and a short Horse is soon wispt.

A fair fire makes a room flet.

A fool may give a wise man a counsell.

A fool when he hes spoken, hes all done.

A fool will not give his Bauble for the Tower of London.

A fools bolt is soon shot.

A foul foot makes a son wemb.

A friend in Court is worth a penny in purse.

A friend is not known but in need.

A friend's Dinner is soon dight.

A full heart lied never.

A full seck will take a clout on the side.

A gangan foot is ay getting, and it were but a thorn.

A gentle Horse would not be over fair spur'd.

A given Horse should not be lookt in the teeth.

A gloved Cat was never a good Hunter.

A good asker should have a good nay-say.

A good beginning makes a good ending.

A good Cow may have an ill Calf.

A good dog never barkt but a bene.

A good fellow tint never, but at an ill fellows hand.

A good Goose indeed, but she hes an ill gansell.

A good piece steil is worth a penny.

A good ruser was never a good rider.

A good word is as soon said as an ill.

A good yeoman makes a good woman.

A greedy man God hates.

A half-penny Cat may look to the King.

A hasty man never wanted woe.

A hearty hand to give a hungry meltith.

A hungry lowse bites fair.

A Lyar should have a good memory.

A Mach and a Horshoe are both alike.

A man cannot thrive except his wife let him.

A man hath no more good then he hath good of.

A man is a Lyon in his own cause.

A man may see his friend need, but will not see him bleed.

A man may speir the gate to Rome.

A man may spit on his hand, and doe full ill.

A man may wooe where he will, but wed where is his weard.

A man that is warned, is half-armed.

A mean pot plaid never even.

A mirk mirrour is a mans mind.

A new Bissom sweeps clean.

A new tout in all old horn.

A poor man is fain of little.

A proud heart in a poor breast, has meikle dolour to dree.

A racklesse hussy makes mony thieves.

A Scots man is ay wife behind band.

A shored Tree stands long.

A silly bairn is eith to lear.

A Skabbed Horse is good enough for a skald Squire.

A skabbed sheep syles ail the flock.

A skade mans head is soon broke.

A sloathfull man is a Beggers brother.

A spoon full of skytter spills a pot full of skins.

A still Sow eats all the Draff.

A tarrowing bairn was never fat.

A teem purse makes a bleat merchant.

A tratler is worse then a thief.

A travelled man hath leave to lye.

A Vaunter and a Lyar is both one thing.

A wight man never wanted a weapon.

A Wool-seller kens a Wool-buyer.

A word before is worth two behinde.

A yeeld Sow was never good to gryses.

A yule feast may be quit at Pasch.

Absence is a shro.

Airly crooks the Tree that good Lammock should be.

All are not maidens that wears bare hair.

All cracks, all beares.

All fails that fools thinks.

All fellows, Jock and the Laird.

All Houndlesse man comes to the best Hunting.

All is not gold that glitters.

All is not in hand that helps.

All is not tint that is in peril.

All is well that ends well.

All overs are ill but over the water.

All the Corn in the Country is not shorn by the Kempers.

All the Keys of the Countrey hangs not at one Belt.

All the speed is in the spurs.

All the winning is in the first buying.

All things are good unseyed.

All things hath a beginning, God excepted.

All things helps quoth the Wran, when she pisht in the Sea.

All things hes an end, a Pudding hes twa.

All things thrive but thrice.

All things wytes that well not fares.

All wald have all, all wald forgive.

Among twenty four fools not ane wise man.

An answer in a word.

An hired Horse tired never.

An Horse may snapper on four feet.

An hungry man sees far.

An ill Cook would have a good Cleaver.

An ill hound comes halting home.

An ill life, an ill end.

An ill servant will never be a good maister.

An ill shearer gat never a good hook.

An ill win penny will cast down a pound.

An ill-willy Cow should have short horns.

An inch of a nag is worth a span of an aver.

An old Knave is na bairn.

An old seck craves meikle clouting.

An old seck is ay skailing.

An oleit Mother makes a fweir Daughter.

An ounce of mother-wit, is worth a pound of clergie.

An unch is a feast, (of Bread and Cheese.)

An unhappy mans Cairt is eith to tumble.

And old hound bytes fair.

Ane Begger is wae, another by the gate gae.

Ane ill word begets another, and it were at at the Bridge at London.

Ane mans meat is another mans poyson.

Ane may lead a Horse to the water, but four and twenty cannot gar him drink.

Ane Swallow makes no summer.

Ane year a Nurish, seven years a Daw.

Anes pay it never crave it.

Anes wood, never wise, ay the worse.

As fair fights Wrans as Cranes.

As fair greits the bairn that is dung after noon, as he that is dung before noon.

As good hads the stirep as he that loups on.

As good haud, as draw.

As good merchant tines as wins.

As long as ye bear the tod, ye man bear up his tail.

As long fives the merry-man, as the wretch for all the craft he can.

As long runs the Fox as he hath feet.

As many heads as many wits.

As meikle upwith, as meikle downwith.

As soon comes the Lamb-skin to the market as the old Sheeps.

As the Carle riches he wretches.

As the fool thinks ay the bell clinks.

As the old Cock craws, the young Cock lears.

As the Sow fills the Draff fowres.

At open doors Dogs come in.

Auld men are twice bairns.

Auld sin, new shame.

Bairns mother burst never.

Bannaks is better nor na kind of bread.

Be the same thing that thou wald be cald.

Bear wealth, poverty will bear itself.

Beauty but bounty avails nought.

Before I wein, and now I wat.

Better a chigging mother, nor a riding father.

Better a clout nor a hole out.

Better a Dog faun nor bark on you.

Better a fowl in hand nor twa flying.

Better a laying Hen nor a lyin Crown.

Better a little fire that warms, nor a meikle that burns.

Better a wit cost, nor two for nought.

Better apple given nor eaten.

Better auld debts nor auld sairs.

Better bairns greit, nor bearded men.

Better be alone nor in ill company.

Better be dead as out of the fashion.

Better be envied nor pittied.

Better be happy nor wise.

Better be well loved, nor ill won geir.

Better bide the Cooks nor the Mediciners.

Better bow nor break.

Better buy as borrow.

Better finger off, nor ay warking.

Better give nor take.

Better good sale, nor good Ale.

Better half an egge, nor teem doup.

Better hand loose, nor bound to an ill baikine.

Better happy to court, nor good service.

Better have a Mouse in the pot as no flesh.

Better held out nor put out.

Better lang little, then soon right nought.

Better late thrive then never.

Better learn by your neighbors skaith nor by your own.

Better leave nor want.

Better never begun nor never endit.

Better no ring, nor the ring of a rash.

Better plays a full wemb nor a new coat.

Better rew sit, nor rew flie.

Better saucht with little aucht, nor care with many cow.

Better say, Here it is, nor, Here it was.

Better sit idle then work for nought.

Better sit stil, nor rise and get a fall.

Better spare at the breird nor at the bottome.

Better two skaiths, nor ane sorrow.

Better unborn nor untaught.

Better wooe over midding, nor over mosse.

Betwixt twae stools the arse falls down.

Beware of Had I wist.

Bind the seck ere it be full.

Binde fast, finde fast.

Biting and scarting is Scots folks Wooing.

Black will be no other Hue.

Blaw the wind nere so saft, it will lowen at the last.

Boden gear stinks.

Bonie silver is soon spendit.

Bourd neither with me, nor with my Honour.

Bourd not with Bawty, fear lest he bite ye.

Breads House skiald never.

Bring a Cow to the Hall, and she will run to the byre again.

Butter and burn-trouts gar maidens f[unreadable] the wind.

Buy when I bid you.

Cadgers speaks of lead saddles.

Calk is na sheares.

Cast not forth the old water while the new come in.

Cats eats that Hussies spares.

Cease your snow balls casting.

Changing of works is lighting of hearts.

Charge your friend ere you need.

Clap a carle on the culs, and he will shit in your louf.

Cold cools the love that kindles over hot.

Come it aire, come it late, in May comes the Cow-quake.

Come not to the councell uncalled.

Comparisons are odious.

Condition makes, and condition breakes.

Court to the Town, and whore to the window.

Crabbit was, and cause had.

Curtesie is cumbersom to them that kens it not.

Cut duels in every Town.

Daffing dow nothing.

Dame dein warily.

Dead and marriage makes Term-day.

Dead at the one door, and heirship at the other.

Dead men bites not.

Dirt parts company.

Do as ye wald be done to.

Do in Hill, as ye wald do in Hall.

Do the likeliest, and God will do the best.

Do weil and have weil.

Do well, and doubt no man; and do weil, and doubt all men.

Dogs will red swine.

Draff is good enough for Swine.

Drink and drouth comes sindle together.

Drive out the inch as thou hast done the span.

Drunken wife gat ay the drunken penny.

Dummie cannot lie.

Early maister, lang knave.

Eat and drink measurely, and defie the mediciners.

Eaten meat is good to pay.

Efter delay comes a Let.

Efter long mint, never dint.

Efter word comes weard.

Eild wald have Honour.

Evening Orts is good morning-fother.

Every land hes his lauch, and every corne hes the caff.

Every man can rule an ill wife, but he that hes Her.

Every man for Himself, quoth the mertine.

Every man slams the fat sows Arse.

Every man wats best where his own shoe binds him.

Every man wisheth the water to his own milne.

Experience may teach a fool.

Fair heights makes fools fain.

Fair words brake never bane, foul words many ane.

Falshood made never a fair Hinder-end.

Far fought, and dear bought, is good for Ladies.

Far fowls have fair feathers.

Few words sufficeth to a wise man.

Fidlers, dogs and flies, come to the feast uncalled.

Fill fow, and had fow, makes a starke man.

Fire is good for the farcy.

Follie is a bonny Dog.

Follow love, and it will flee from thee; leave it, and it will follow thee.

Fool hast is no speed.

Fools are fain of flitting.

Fools are fain of right nought.

Fools make feasts, and wise men eat them.

Fools set far trystes.

Fools should have no chappin sticks.

For a tint thing care not.

For fault of wise men fools sits on binks.

For love of the Nuris, many kisses the Bairn.

Forbid a fool a thing, and that he will do.

Foul water slokens fire.

Freedome is a fair thing.

Friendship stands not in One side.

Giff, gaff, makes good friends.

Girne when you knit, and laugh when ye loose.

Give never the Wolf the Wedder to keep.

Go to the Devil for Gods-sake.

God sends meat, and the Devil sends Cooks.

God sends men cold, as they have clothes to.

God sends never the mouth, but the meat with it.

Gods help is nearer nor the fair even.

Goe shoe the Geese.

Good chear, and good cheap, garres many haunt the House.

Good wine needs not a wisp.

Good-will should be tane in part of payment.

Grace is best for the man.

Had-I-fish, was never good with Garlick.

Hair, and hair, makes the Carles head bare.

Hald in geir, helps well.

Half a nuch is half sill.

Half a tale is enough to a wise man.

Hall-binks are fliddery.

Hame is hamely, though never so seemly.

Hanging gangs by hap.

Hap and an halfpennie is worlds geir enough.

Happy man, happy cavil.

Hast makes wast.

Have God and have All.

He calls me scabbed, because I will not call him skade.

He gangs early to steal, that cannot say Na.

He hes wit at will, that with angry heart can hold him still.

He is a fairy beggar that may not goe by ane mans door.

He is a fairy Cook, that may not lick his own fingers.

He is a proud Tod that will not scrape his own Hole.

He is a weak Horse that may not bear the Saddle.

He is blind that eats his marrow, but far blinder that lets him.

He is fairest dung when his own wand dings him.

He is good that fail'd never.

He is not the best Wright that hews the maniest speals.

He is not the fool that the fool is, but he that with the fool deals.

He is poor that God Hates.

He is twise fain, that sits on a slane.

He is well easit that hes ought of his own, when others go to meat.

He is well staikit thereben, that will neither borrow, nor len.

He is wise who can make a friend of a foe.

He is wise, that is ware in time.

He is wise, when he is well can had him sa.

He is worth no weil that may bide no wae.

He loves me for little that hates me for nought.

He mon have leave to speak that cannot had his tongue.

He plaints early that plaints on his kail.

He rides sicker that fell never.

He rises over early that is hangit ere noon.

He should have a heal pow, that cals his neighbour nikkynow.

He should have a long shafted spoon that sups kail with the Devil.

He should wear iron shone, that bides his neighbours deed.

He sits above that deals aikers.

He sits full still that hes a riven brick.

He that blaws best bears away the Horn.

He that borrows and bigs; makes feasts and thigs; drinks and is not dry; these three are not thrifty.

He that comes first to the hill, may sit where he will.

He that comes un-call'd sits un-serv'd.

He that counts all costs, will never put plow in the yeard.

He that counts but his Host, counts twise.

He that crabs without cause, should mease without mends.

He that does bidding, deserves na dinging.

He that does his turn in time, sits half idle.

He that does ill hates the light.

He that eats while he lasts, will be the war while he die.

He that evill does, never good weins.

He that fishes afore the net, long e're he fish get.

He that forsakes missour, missour forsake him.

He that hes gold may buy land.

He that hes no geir to tine, hes shins to pine.

He that hes twa huirds, is able to get the third.

He that hews over hie, the spail will fall into his eye.

He that is evil deem'd is half hang'd.

He that is far from his geir, is near his skaith.

He that is fraid of a far [unreadable] should never hear thunder.

He that is hated of his subjects, cannot be counted a King.

He that is ill of his harbery, is good of his way kenning.

He that is red for windlestraws, should not sleep in lees.

He that is welcome fares well.

He that lippens to bon plows, his land will ly ley.

He that looks not e're he loup, will fall e're he wit of himself.

He that marries a Daw, eats meikle dirt.

He that marries e're he be wise, will die e're he thrive.

He that may not do as he would, mon do as he may.

He that owes the Cow goes nearest her tail.

He that shames, shall be shemt.

He that slayes, shall be slain.

He that spares to speak, spares to speed.

He that speaks the things he should not, hears the things he would not.

He that spends his geir on a whore, hes both shame and skaith.

He that takes all his geir fra himself, and gives it to his bairns, it were weil ward to take a mell and knock out his hairns.

He that tholes, overcomes.

He that was born to be hang'd will never be drown'd.

He that will not hear motherhead, shall hear stepmotherhead.

He that will not when he may, shalt not when he wald.

He tint never a Cow, that grat for a needle.

He was scant of news, that told his father was hang'd.

Hea, will gar a deaf man hear.

Hear all parties.

Help thy self, and God will help thee.

Honesty is na pride.

Hoordom and grace, can never bide in one place.

Huly and fair men rides far journeys.

Hunger is good Kitchir-meat.

Hunger is hard in a heal man.

Hunting, hawking, and paramours, for one joy an hundred displeasures.

I cannot find you both tails and ears.

I have a good bow, but it is in the Castle.

I have a sliddery Eel by the tail.

I have seen as light a green.

I shall hold his Nose to the Grindstone.

I shall sit on his skirt.

I wat where my own shoe binds me.

I would I had as meikle pepper as he counts himself worthy Mice dirt.

If a man knew what would be dear, he would be but Merchant for a year.

If ane will not, another will.

If ever ye make a lucky pudding, I shall eat the prick.

If God be with us, who will be against us.

If he may spend meikle, put the more to the fire.

If he steal not my kail, break not my dike.

If I can get his cart at a Waltar, I shall lend it a put.

If I may not keep geese, I shall keep gesline.

If thou do no ill, do no ill like.

If ye wanted me, and your meat, you would want ane good friend.

Ilk a man as he loves, let him send to the Cooks,

Ilk man mend ane, and all will be mendit.

Ill bairns are best heard at home.

Ill herds makes fat wolfes.

Ill weeds waxes weil.

Ill win, ill warit.

In a good time I speak it, in a better I leave it.

In some mens aught mon the old horse die.

In space, comes Grace.

It goes as meiklle in his heart, as in his heel.

It goes in at one ear, and out at the other.

It hes neither [unreadable], nor elbow.

It is a bare Moor that he goes over, and gets not a Cow.

It is a fair feild where all are dung down.

It is a fairy brewing that is not good in the newing.

It is a fairy collop that is tane off a Capon.

It is a good Goose that drops ay.

It is a pain both to pay and pray.

It is a silly flock where the yow bears the bell.

It is a sin to lye on the Devil.

It is a sooth board that men sees wakin.

It is as meet as a Sow to bear a Saddle.

It is as meet as a thief for the widdie.

It is dear bought honey that is lickt off a thorn.

It is eich to cry yule on another man's cost;

It is eith till, that the awn self will.

It is eith to swim where the head is hild up.

It is fair in the hall, when beards wag all.

It is good baking besides meal.

It is good fishing in drumbling waters.

It is good mows that fills the wemb.

It is good sleeping in a heal skin.

It is hard to fling at the brod, or kick at the prick.

It is hard to wive and thrive in a year.

It is ill to bring but the thing that is not thereben.

It is ill to bring out of the flesh that is bred in the bene.

It is ill to draw a strea before an old Cat.

It is ill to make a bowing horn of a tods tail.

It is ill to take a breik off a bare [unreadable].

It is ill to waken sleeping dogs.

It is kindly that the poke fair of the Herring.

It is little of God's might, to make a poor man a Knight.

It is na mair pitty to see a Woman greit, nor to see a Goose go barefoot.

It is na play where ane greits, and another laughs.

It is na time to stoup when the head is off.

It is not good to want, and to have.

It is not the habit that makes the Monck.

It is not tint that is done to friends.

It is short while seen the louse boore the langelt.

It is true that all men sayes.

It is weil warit that wasters warn geir.

It is weil warit they have sorrow, that buyes it with their silver.

It is well said, but who will bell the Cat?

It that God will give, the Devil cannot reave.

It that lies not in your gate, breaks not your shins.

It will be an ill web to bleitch.

It will come in an hour, that will not come in a year.

It's a cold coal to blow at.

It's a fair dung bairn that dare not greit.

It's a silly pack that may not pay the custom.

It's tint that is done to old men and bairns.

Kail spares bread.

Kame single, kame fair.

Kamesters are ay creeshie.

Kindnesse cannot be bought for geir.

Kindnesse comes of will.

Kindnesse lies not ay in ane side of the house.

Kindnesse will creep where it may not gang.

Kings and Bears oft worries their Keepers.

Kings are out of play.

Kings caff is worth other mens corn.

Kings have a long ears.

Knowledge is eith born about.

Lads will be men.

Laith to bed, laith out of it.

Laith to the drink, laith fra it.

Last in bed, best heard.

Lata is long and dreigh.

Laugh, and lay down again.

Lear young, lear fair.

Leave the Court, ere the Court leave thee.

Let alone makes many lurden.

Let him drink as he hes browen.

Let them that are cold blow at the coal.

Light supper makes long life.

Light winning makes a heavy purse.

Lightly comes, lightly goes.

Like draws to like, a skabbed Horse to an old dyke.

Like to die mends not the Kirkyard.

Liked geir is half bought.

Likely lies in the mire, and unlikely goes by it.

Lips go, laps go, he that eats, let him pay.

Little intermitting makes good friends.

Little kens the wife that sits by the fire, how the wind blows cold in hurle-burle swyre.

Little may an old Horse do, if he may not neigh.

Little sayd is soon mended, and a little geir is soon spended.

Little troubles the eye, but far lesse the soul.

Little wars an ill hussie what a dinner holds in.

Little wit makes meikle travel.

Live, and let live.

Livelesse, faultlesse.

Long ere you cut Falkland-wood with a Pen-knife.

Long lean wakes hameald cattell.

Long standing, and little offering, makes a poor price.

Long tarrowing takes all the thank away.

Lordships changes manners.

Love hes no lack.

Love me little, and love me long.

Love me, love my dog.

Lucke and bone voyage.

Maidens should be meek while they be married.

Maistery mowes the Meadows down.

Make no balks of good beerland.

Make not meikle of little.

Make not twa mewes of ane daughter.

Man propones, but God dispones.

Many Aunts, many Eames, many kin, and few friends.

Many brings the rake, but few the shovel.

Many cares for meal that has baken bread enough.

Many do lack, that yet would fain have in their pack.

Many hands makes light work.

Many irons in the fire, pare must cool.

Many maisters, quoth the Poddock to the Harrow, when every tind took her a knock.

Many man makes an errand to the hall to bid the Lady good-day.

Many man serves a thanklesse master.

Many man speirs the gate he kens full well.

Many purses holds friends together.

Many smalls makes a great.

Many speaks of Robin Hood, that never shot in his Bow.

Many tines the half-mark whinger for the half-penny whang.

Many words fills not the furlot.

Many words would have meikle drink.

March Whisquer was never a good Fisher.

Measure, is Treasure.

Meat and Masse, never hindred man.

Meat is good, but Mense is better.

Meat makes, and clothes shapes, but manners makes a man.

Meikle has, would ay have more.

Meikle Head, little Wit.

Meikle must a good heart thole.

Meikle spoken, part must spill.

Men are blind in their own cause.

Men goes over the dike at the laichest.

Men may buy Gold over dear.

Mends is worth misdeeds.

Messengers should neither be headed nor hanged.

Mickle Water runs, where the Miller sleeps.

Might oftentimes overcomes right.

Millers take ay the best Multar with their own Hand.

Mint, ere ye strike.

Mister makes men of craft.

Misterfull folk must not be mensfull.

Musle not the Oxens mouth.

Mustard after meat.

Na man can both sup and blow together.

Nature passes Nurture.

Need gars naked men run, and sorrow gars Websters spin.

Need hes no law.

Need makes Virtue.

Neir is the Kirtle, but neirer is the Sark.

Neirest the heart, neirest the mouth.

Neirest the King, neirest the Widdie.

Neirest to the Kirk, farthest fra God.

Never rade, never fell.

New Lords, new Laws.

No man can play the fool so well as the wise man.

No man can seek his marrow in the Kirn, so weil as he that hes bin in it himself.

No man makes his own hap.

No man may puind for unkindnesse.

No penny, no pardon.

No plea is best.

Nothing comes sooner to light, than that which is long hid.

Nothing enters a close Hand.

Nothing is difficile to a weill willed man.

Of all War, Peace is the final end.

Of ane ill comes many.

Of enough, men leave.

Of ill Debtois men takes Oattes.

Of need make Virtue.

Of other mens leather, men take large whangs.

Of the abundance of the heart the mouth speaketh.

Of the Earth mon the dike be biggit.

Of two ills choose the least.

Oft counting makes good friends.

Out of sight, out of langer.

Over fast, over loose.

Over great familiarity genders despight.

Over high, over laigh.

Over hot, over cold.

Over jolly dow not.

Over meikle of any thing is good for nothing.

Over narrow counting culzies no kindnesse.

Painters and Poets may have leave to lie.

Patience perforce.

Penny wise, pound fool.

Peter in, and Paul out.

Pith is good in all Playes.

Play with your peers.

Plenty, is na Dainty.

Poor men (they say) have no souls.

Poor men are fain of little thing.

Possession is worth an ill chartour.

Poverty parts good company, and is an enemy to vertue.

Preists and Doves, make foul houses.

Pride and sweirnesse would have meikle upholding.

Pride will have a fall.

Provision in season makes a rich meason.

Puddings and Paramours would be hotly handled.

Put a begger on horseback, and he will ride fast, or else break his neck.

Put not your hand betwixt the rind and the Tree.

Put that in the next few.

Put twa half-pennies in a purse, and they will draw together.

Put your hand into the creel, and you will get either an adder, or an Eele.

Put your hand no farther nor your sleeve may reek.

Qhuen thieves reckons, leal men comes to their geir.

Quha may hold that will away?

Quha may wooe, but Cost?

Quhair stands your great horse?

Quhair the Deer is slain, some bloud will lie.

Quhair the Pig breaks, let the shels lie.

Quhat better is the house that the Daw rises in the morning.

Quhen a man is full of lust, his wemb is full of leasing.

Quhen all men speaks, no man hears.

Quhen friends meets, hearts warms.

Quhen I am dead, make me a caddel.

Quhen Taylours are true, there is little good to shew.

Quhen the belly is full the bones would be at rest.

Quhen the craw flees, her tail follows.

Quhen the cup is fullest, bear it evenest.

Quhen the eye sees not, the heart rewes not.

Quhen the good-man is fra hame, the board-cloth is tint.

Quhen the good-wife is fra hame, the keys are tint.

Quhen the iron is hot, it is time to strike.

Quhen the Play is best, it is best to lear.

Quhen the Steed is stoon, steik the stable-door.

Quhen the Tod preaches, beware of the hens.

Quhen the well is full, it will run over.

Quhen thy neighbours house is on fire, take tent to thy own.

Quhen wine is in, wits out.

Quhiles the hawk hes, and whiles he hunger hes.

Quhiles thou, whiles I, soe goes the Baillerie.

Quhom God will help, no man can hinder.

Racklesse youth makes a goustie Age.

Reason band the man.

Reavers should not be rewers.

Rhue and time, grows both in ane garden.

Rome was not bigged on the first Day.

Rule youth well, and eild will rule it fell.

Ruse the fair day at even.

Ruse the Ford, as ye find it.

Ryme spares no man.

Sain you will fra the Devil, and the Lairds bairns.

Sairy be your meil-poke, and ay your nieve in the nook on't.

Saw thin, and maw thin.

Scots-men reckon ay fra an ill hour.

Seek your sauce where you get your Ale.

Seil comes not while sorrow be gone.

Seldom lies the Devil dead by the dike side.

Seldom rides, tynes the spurres.

Self do, self ha.

Send him to the sea and he will not get water.

Send, and fetch.

Seying goes good cheap.

Shame is past the shad of your haire.

Shame shall fall them that shame thinks, to do themselves a good turn.

She hath past the discipline of a Tavern.

She is a sairy mouse, that hes but one Hole.

She that takes gifts her self, she sels; and she that gives, does nought else.

She's a foul bird that syles her own nest.

Shew me the man, and I will shew you the Law.

Shod in the cradle, bair-foot in the Stubble.

Shro the ghuest the house is the war of.

Sike a man as thou would be, draw thee to sike company.

Sike answer as a man gives, sike will he get.

Sike father, sike son.

Sike lippes, sike Latace.

Sike man, sike master.

Sike Priest, sike Offering.

Small winning makes a heavy purse.

Soft fire makes sweet malt.

Sokeing sale is best.

Soon gotten, soon spended.

Soon ripe, soon rotten.

Sooth bourd is na bourd.

Speir at Jock-thief my marrow, if I be a leal man.

Spit on the Stane, and it will be wet at the last.

Sturt payes na Debt.

Surfeit slayes mae nor the sword,

Swear by your brunt shins.

Take a man by his word, and a Cow by her horn.

Take him up there with his five Egges, and four of them rotten.

Take part of the pelf when the pack is a dealing.

Take time while time is, for time will away.

Tarrowing bairns were never fat.

Teem bags rattles.

That which hussies spares, Cats eat.

The blind Horse is hardiest.

The Craw thinks her awn Bird fairest.

The day hes eyne, the night hes ears.

The goose-pan is above the roast.

The grace of God is geir enough.

The greatest Clerks are not the wisest men.

The higher up, the greater fall.

The lesse play the better.

The longer we live, the more farlies we see.

The mae the merrier, the fewer the better cheer.

The mair cost, the mair honour.

The mair haste, the war speed.

The Malt is above the Meal.

The more ye tramp in a [unreadable] it grows the broader.

The mother of mischief is na mair nor a midgewing.

The mouth that lyes, slayes the foul.

The next time ye dance, wit whom ye take by the hand.

The Piper wants meikle, that wants the nether chafts.

The shots overgoes the old swine.

The Sowter's wife is worst shod.

The Tailours wife is worst clad.

The thing that is fristed, is not forgiven.

The tree falls not at the first strake.

The weakest goes to the walls.

The worst world that ever was, some man wan.

There are mae maidens, nor maukin.

There are mae wayes to the wood nor ane.

There are many fair words in the marriage making, but few in the tochergood paying.

There are many sooth words spoken in bourding.

There belongs mair to a bed nor four bare leggs.

There came never a large Fart forth of a Wrans [unreadable].

There came never ill of good Advisement.

There is a dog in the well.

There is little sap in dry peis hools.

There is little to the rake to get after the beisome.

There is many a fair thing full false.

There is meikle between word and deed.

There is meikle hid meat in a Goose eye.

There is na man so deaf as he that will not hear.

There is na thief without a Resetter.

There is no fool to an old fool.

There is no friend, to a friend in mister.

There is no medicine for fear.

There is none without a fault.

There is nothing mair precious nor time.

There is nothing so crouse, as a new washen louse.

There is remead for all things but starke dead.

There was never a Cake, but it had a make.

There was never a fair word in flyting.

They are as wife, as speir not.

They are good willy of their Horse that hes none.

They are lightly herrite, that hes all their awn.

They are welcome that brings.

They buy good cheap that brings nothing hame.

They had never an ill day, that had a good evening.

They laugh ay that wins.

They mense little the mouth, that bites off the nose.

They put at the Cairt, that is ay gangan.

They that speirs meikle will get wot of part.

They were never fain that fidgit.

They will know by an half-penny if a Preist will take offering.

This bolt came never out of your bag.

This world will not last ay.

Thou shouldst not tell thy foe when thy foot sleeps.

Thou wilt get no more of the cat, but the skin.

Thraw the wand while it is green.

Three may keep counsel if twa be away.

Thy Thumb is under my Belt.

Thy tongue is no slander.

Tide and time, bides na man.

Time tries the truth.

Touch a gall'd Horse on the back and he will fling.

Touch me not on the fair heel.

Tread on a Worm and she will stir her tail.

Trot mother, trot father, how should the foal amble?

True love kythes in time of need.

Twa Daughters, and a back-door, are three stark thieves.

Twa hungry meltithes makes the third a glutton.

Twa wits is better nor ane.

Two fools in ane house, is over many.

Two Wolves may worry ane Sheep.

Unskilfull mediciners, and horse-marshels slayes, both man and beast.

Use makes perfectnesse.

Use your friend as ye would have him.

Waken not sleeping dogs.

Wark bears witnesse who weil does.

We have a craw to pluck.

We hounds flew the Hare, quoth the messoun.

Wealth gars wit waver.

Weapons bodes peace.

Weil bides, weil betides.

Weil is that weil does.

Weil worth aw, that gars the plough draw.

Well done, soon done.

Well good-mother-daughter.

Whatrax my Jo, I ken your coptan.

Whatrax of the seed, where the frendship dow not.

Wiles help weak folk.

Wishers and woulders are poor householders.

Wit in a poor mans head, and mosse in a mountain, avails nothing.

With empty hand no man should hawks allure.

Women and bairns keep counsell of that they ken not.

Wonder lasts but nine nights in a Town.

Wont beguil'd the Lady.

Wood in wildernesse, and strength in a fool.

Words are but winde, but dunts are the Devill.

Wrang hearing makes wrang rehearsing.

Wrang hes no warrand.

Wrong count is no payment.

Ye breed of the cat, ye would fain have fish, but ye have na will to wet your feet.

Ye breed of the gouk, ye have not a rime but ane.

Ye breed of the Millers dog, ye lick your lips ere the poke be open.

Ye cannot make a silk purse of a sows lug.

Ye drive a Snail to Rome.

Ye have a face to God, and another to the Devil.

Ye have a ready mouth for a ripe cherry.

Ye learn your Father to get bairns.

Ye may drink of the burn, but not bite of the brae.

Ye may not sit in Rome, and strive with the Pope.

Ye may puind for debt, but not for unkindnesse.

Ye ride a bootlesse errand.

Ye seek grace at a gracelesse face.

Ye seek hot water under cold ice.

Ye should be a King of your word.

Ye strive against the stream.

Ye will break your crag as soon as your fast in his house.

Ye will get war bodes ere Beltan.

Ye would doe little for God, and the Devil were dead.

Your winning is no my tinsel.

Youth and age will never agree.

Youth never casts for peril.

# 8 Celtic Lyrics

This book would not be complete without the inclusion of three special songs that are near dear to the heart of the young lady to whom this book is dedicated.

## Finnegan's Wake
### (Ronnie Drew & the Dubliner's Version)

Ah Tim Finnegan lived in Walkin Street
A gentleman Irish mighty odd
Well, he had a tongue both rich and sweet
An' to rise in the world he carried a hod
Ah but Tim had a bit of a tippler's way
With the love of the liquor he was born
An' to send him on his way each day
He'd a drop of the craythur every morn!

Whack fol the dah will ya dance to yer partner
Around the flure with yer trotters shake
Wasn't it the truth I told you?
Lots of fun at Finnegan's Wake!

One morning Tim was rather full
His head felt heavy, which made him shake
He fell off the ladder and he broke his skull
And they carried him home his corpse to wake

143

Well, they rolled him up in a nice clean sheet
And they laid him out upon the bed
With a bottle of whiskey at his feet
And a barrel of porter at his head!

Whack fol the dah will ya dance to yer partner
Around the flure with yer trotters shake
Isn't it the truth I tell you?
Lots of fun at Finnegan's Wake!

Well his friends assembled at the wake
And Mrs. Finnegan called for lunch
Well first they brought in tay and cake
Then pipes, tobacco and brandy punch
Then the widow Malone did began to cry
"Such a lovely corpse, did you ever see,
Arrah, Tim avourneen, why did you die?"
"Will ye hould your gob?" said Molly McGee!

Whack fol the dah will ya dance to yer partner
Around the flure with yer trotters shake
Isn't it the truth I tell you?
Lots of fun at Finnegan's Wake!

Well Mary O'Connor took up the job
"Biddy" says she "you're wrong, I'm sure"
Well Biddy gave her a belt in the gob
And left her sprawling on the floor
Well civil war did then engage
T'was woman to woman and man to man
Shillelagh law was all the rage
And a row and a ruction soon began!

Whack fol the dah will ya dance to yer partner
Around the flure with yer trotters shake
Isn't it the truth I tell you?
Lots of fun at Finnegan's Wake

Well Tim Maloney raised his head
When a bottle of whiskey flew at him
He ducked, and landing on the bed
The whiskey scattered over Tim
Bedad he revives, see how he rises
Tim Finnegan rising in the bed
Saying "Whittle your whiskey around like blazes
T'underin' Jaysus, did ye think I was dead?"

Whack fol the dah will ya dance to yer partner
Around the flure with yer trotters shake
Wasn't it the truth I told you?
Lots of fun at Finnegan's Wake!

---

## The Mountain Dew
*(One of Many Versions)*

Let grasses grow and waters flow
In a free and easy way
But give me enough of the rare old stuff
That's made near Galway Bay
And policemen all from Donegal,
Sligo and Leitrim too
We'll give them the slip and we'll take a sip
Of the real old mountain dew.

Skidly-idle-diddle-dum
Skidly-idle-diddle-dum
Skidly-idle-diddle-diddle-dum-day
Skidly-idle-diddle-dum
Skidly-idle-diddle-dum
Skidly-idle-dum-diddle-dum-day

There's a neat little still at the foot of the hill
Where the smoke curls up to the sky
By a whiff of the smell you can plainly tell

That there's poitin, boys, close by.
For it fills the air with a perfume rare
And betwixt both me and you
As home we roll, we can drink a bowl
Or a bucketful of mountain dew.

Skidly-idle-diddle-dum
Skidly-idle-diddle-dum
Skidly-idle-diddle-diddle-dum-day
Skidly-idle-diddle-dum
Skidly-idle-diddle-dum
Skidly-idle-dum-diddle-dum-day

Now learned men as use the pen
Have writ' the praises high
Of the rare poitin from Ireland green
Distilled from wheat and rye
Away with your pills, it'll cure all ills
Be ye pagan, Christian, or Jew
So take off your coat and grease your throat
With a bucket of the mountain dew.

Skidly-idle-diddle-dum
Skidly-idle-diddle-dum
Skidly-idle-diddle-diddle-dum-day
Skidly-idle-diddle-dum
Skidly-idle-diddle-dum
Skidly-idle-dum-diddle-dum-day

---

# The Unicorn Song
*(The Irish Rovers Version)*

A long time ago, when the Earth was green,
There was more kinds of animals than you've ever seen.
And they'd run around free when the Earth was being born,
And the loveliest of 'em all was the unicorn.

There was green alligators and long-necked geese,
Some humpty backed camels and some chimpanzees.
Some cats and rats and elephants, but sure as you're born,
The loveliest of all was the unicorn.

Well now God seen some sinnin' and it caused Him pain.
And He said, "Stand back, I'm going to make it rain!"
He said, "Hey, Brother Noah, I'll tell you what to do,
build me a floating zoo,"

"and take some of them" .......

"Green alligators and long-necked geese,
Some humpty backed camels and some chimpanzees.
Some cats and rats and elephants, but sure as you're born.
Don't you forget My unicorns."

Well, Old Noah he was there, and he answered the callin',
And he finished makin' the ark just as the rain started to fallin'.
Then he marched in all them animals two by two,
And he sung out as they went through,

"Hey Lord,"

"I got Your green alligators and long-necked geese,
Some humpty backed camels and some chimpanzees.
Some cats and rats and elephants, but Lord, I'm so forlorn,
I just can't see no unicorns !"

And Noah looked out through the driving rain,
The unicorns were hiding, playing sally games.
They were kickin' and splashin' while the rain was pourin',
Oh, the sally unicorns!

There was green alligators and long-necked geese,
Some humpty backed camels and some chimpanzees.
Noah cried, "Close the door 'cause the rain is just pourin',
And we just cannot wait for no unicorn!"

The ark started moving, and it drifted with the tide,
And the unicorns looked up from the rocks and they cried.
And the waters come down and sort of flooded them away,
That's why you never seen a unicorn to this very day.

But you'll see green alligators and long-necked geese,
Some humpty backed camels and some chimpanzees.
Some cats and rats and elephants, but sure as you're born,
You're never gonna see no unicorn!

# About the Author

The Author was born and reared in the Highlands of East Tennessee, originally settled for the most part by immigrants to America from Scotland and Ireland. He is a descendant on both sides of the Clan Campbell and several dozen other Scottish Clans.

Through his Clan Campbell heritage, he is descendant from Alfred the Great of Saxon England, the Kings of Scotland, the ancient Kings of Ireland, the Dukes of Normandy, the Jarls and Kings of the Norse, and the Chiefs of Clan Sinclair and Knights Templar of Rosslyn.

He is a member of the Clan Campbell Society of North America and encourages all he meets to research, learn and understand their ancestral roots amd family heritage...what ever they may be. You NEVER know what you might find!

He is an author, graphic artist by trade, Freemason and proprietor of the Masonic Press.

Visit us online for many unique, useful and interesting books:

# masonicpress.com

# NE OBLIVISCARIS!
### (Do Not Forget!)

Motto of the Clan Campbell,
The Celts of the
Western Scottish Highlands

22835941R00090

Printed in Great Britain
by Amazon